T0330667

# History of PR in Canada

A first of its kind, this annotated bibliography provides an overview of the development of public relations research in the Canadian context.

A valuable resource for researchers, students or practitioners, this bibliography surveys the landscape of public relations research in Canada. It orientates readers to this unique history, identifies gaps in research, suggests topics of future research and offers critical historiography. This reference work will be of interest to scholars, students and practitioners in the fields of strategic communications, marketing or communications, providing a greater understanding of communications research in various Canadian contexts such as government, industry, corporate and nonprofit.

**Sandra L. Braun** is an associate professor of public relations at Mount Royal University. Her research interests are PR pedagogy, PR history and PR in the Canadian context. She makes her home in Calgary, Alberta, near the palatial peaks of Canada's Rocky Mountains.

**Ella Palin** studied history at Durham University, UK. Pursuing a career in academia, her research areas specialise in political intellectual history and long-run economic developments. She has written for a global trade journal looking at current and historical economic and political developments.

**Hannah Farrow** studied history at Durham University, UK, with specific interests in North American and intellectual history, particularly regarding the development of scientific thought and how this informed the construction of modern society. Her professional interest is risk and compliance which she will pursue in her graduate Public Sector Assurance role whilst studying for the level 7 Chartered Accountancy qualification.

## History of Public Relations: A Global Approach

Series Editors: Dr Anastasios Theofilou is Principal Academic in Public Relations in the Faculty of Media and Communication of Bournemouth University.

Professor Tom Watson PhD is Emeritus Professor of Public Relations in the Faculty of Media and Communication of Bournemouth University.

The history of public relations has received limited attention over the years, as researchers and practitioners struggle to classify historical themes in PR. This series incorporates books focusing on the most popular historical themes in the field of public relations.

As a collection, this series is a major contribution to the history and historiography of PR, creating new knowledge and providing fresh perspectives for researchers, advanced students, and reflective practitioners.

*The History of Public Relations: A Global Approach* series is for:

- researchers of marketing communications disciplines with a focus in communication, PR or political communication
- advanced students of marketing communications disciplines with a major in communication or PR
- academics in the field of communication who are interested in teaching or researching PR
- practitioners wishing to understand the history of PR in order to enrich their practice of the discipline.

**Women in PR History**
*Edited by Anastasios Theofilou*

**History of PR in Canada**
An Annotated Bibliography and Critical Historiography of Public Relations Research in Canada
*Sandra L. Braun, Ella Palin and Hannah Farrow*

For more information about this series, please visit: www.routledge.com/series/HPR

# History of PR in Canada

An Annotated Bibliography and
Critical Historiography of Public
Relations Research in Canada

**Sandra L. Braun, Ella Palin and
Hannah Farrow**

LONDON AND NEW YORK

First published 2025
by Routledge
4 Park Square, Milton Park, Abingdon, Oxon OX14 4RN

and by Routledge
605 Third Avenue, New York, NY 10158

*Routledge is an imprint of the Taylor & Francis Group, an informa business*

*British Library Cataloguing-in-Publication Data*
A catalogue record for this book is available from the British Library

ISBN: 978-1-032-83042-1 (hbk)
ISBN: 978-1-032-83043-8 (pbk)
ISBN: 978-1-003-50747-5 (ebk)

DOI: 10.4324/9781003507475

Typeset in Times New Roman
by Apex CoVantage, LLC

# Contents

# Preface and Acknowledgements

This is the book I wished I had had when I began my academic career at a Canadian university some years ago. I saw that PR and strategic communications scholarship in the Canadian context was limited, scattered and unheralded. I scoured whatever literature I could find, scholarly or industry, that would orient me about PR in Canada, whether its history, evolution, development or status.

As I engaged in this pursuit through the years, my understanding of the PR and strategic communications picture in Canada grew, and a clearer image began to emerge. At some point, I realised I had assembled a set of knowledge that could be shared. This knowledge, combined with a more systematic review of databases, peppered with some critique and observations, provides the basis for *History of PR in Canada: An Annotated Bibliography and Critical Historiography of Public Relations Research in Canada*. It is a collection of research articles, books, textbooks, archival sources and industry reports that illuminates PR research and practice in the Canadian context. While it is extensive, it is not necessarily exhaustive. It is meant not only to inform but to offer some clarity about the historical development of PR research in Canada and identify possible future research directions. Therefore, it serves both as a muster point and a launching pad.

This annotated bibliography is prepared for, and dedicated to, PR and strategic communications researchers who have interest in the Canadian context, wherever they may be. It is for formal academics, industry-based practitioners, graduate students or undergraduate students; it is for those who are established, rising through the ranks, or who will emerge in the future. May you find this helpful on your journey, and may you greatly add to the literature about PR in Canada.

I thank Ella Palin and Hannah Farrow from Durham University, England, who conducted extensive research and did the hard work of drafting summaries. I also thank Lachlan Burr, graduate of Mount Royal University's PR program, for the specific review of articles published in Canadian communications journals.

This work was supported through a grant by the Mitacs Global Research Internship program awarded by the Government of Canada.

Sandra L. Braun

# Abbreviations and Acronyms Used

AEJMC   Association for Education in Journalism and Mass Communication
CBC     Canadian Broadcasting Corporation
CEO     Chief Executive Officer
CPRS    Canadian Public Relations Society
CRTC    Canadian Radio-television and Communications Commission
CSR     corporate social responsibility
DEI     diversity, equity and inclusion
GAP     Generally Accepted Practices
IABC    International Association of Business Communicators
NGOs    non-governmental organisations
OPR     organisation-public relationship
PR      public relations
PRSA    Public Relations Society of America
RACE    Research, Action and planning, Communication, Evaluation
        (Model)
RBC     Royal Bank of Canada
RSS     Really Simple Syndication or Rich Site Summary
U.S.    United States
WWII    World War II; the Second World War

# Part One

# Introduction

# Introduction

This annotated bibliography provides a historical marker – a benchmark in time – about the status of the development of PR practice and scholarship within the country context of Canada.

It is based on the *national histories movement* approach of the study of PR history (Meyers, 2021) that recognises the examination of PR history as contextualised by regional, cultural and societal factors, forged under unique national circumstances.

This monograph, therefore, presents a collection of PR scholarship, sources and key reports about PR in the Canadian context from the past to the present. The first attempt to capture and document the status of Canadian PR scholarship was by Ferguson (1993). This annotated bibliography formalises and updates this line of enquiry; it can be used for information, study or to point to future research directions, particularly to develop new narratives of PR development in the Canadian context (Thurlow, 2015).

The discussion regarding exploration of Canadian distinctions in the Canadian context was supported by this author, Sandra Braun, in a research proposal to *Canadian + Public Relations Foundation* outlining the need for such studies (Barbara Sheffield, email communication, June 30, 2013). An additional recommendation was made by this author to CPRS, calling for Canadian participation in the GAP Study (a study of PR in different countries), created by researchers at Annenberg School for Communication and Journalism at University of Southern California (Richard Truscott and Karen Dalton, email communication, May 24, 2013). Participating countries at the time included Australia, New Zealand, Brazil, South Africa and the United States. This idea came to fruition, and the Canadian portion of the research was executed by researchers at Mount Saint Vincent University, who produced an important benchmark study (Thurlow et al., 2014).

## Method

This book contains 235 annotated bibliographic entries. These were obtained by utilising search terms *public relations*, *Canada*, *public relations history*,

DOI: 10.4324/9781003507475-2

*Canadian* and/or *strategic communication* contained within the title and/or subject terms of publications in academic databases, Google Scholar and WorldCat.

This yielded some 700 resources. Peer-reviewed sources (particularly books, textbooks and journal articles) were primarily selected. Industry sources were considered for their significance; for example, *firsts*, such as the first report on diversity, equity and inclusion (DEI) in PR sponsored by CPRS (2021).

Serial industry publications (e.g., newsletters, magazines, trade articles, white papers) were not generally included due to limited publication space; however, some of these sources may have been included for historical interest such as very early government and industry publications. (Also, historical sources can be particularly revealing in charting the development of the field, and reveal certain uniquenesses.)

This monograph does not include the many industry-based studies conducted by Canadian practitioners in the course of pursuing professional accreditation through CPRS. This is a unique collection housed in the CPRS archives at Mount Royal University in Calgary, Alberta, which could form the basis of other studies.

The 700 sources were analysed individually for relevance and duplication and culled to 234 entries. These were summarised and annotated by a team of three researchers including the principal investigator, a Canadian with 35 combined years of experience in industry and in academia.

The annotations are written primarily as brief *descriptions* and include any *evaluative critique* as to how the source may inform or represent the development of the PR industry, practice or education in Canada.

## Structure of the Book

The 234 annotations are divided into decade groupings as chapters. Chapter 2 covers the period 1930s–1970s (n=10); Chapter 3, 1980s (n=10); Chapter 4, 1990s (n=20); Chapter 5, 2000s (n=59); Chapter 6, 2010s (n=107); Chapter 7, 2020s (n=28). Within each chapter, annotations are listed chronologically by year, and then alphabetically by author within each year in the style of the American Psychological Association, a common citation style in PR industry and scholarship. At the beginning of each chapter is a summative evaluation of any notable developments of the period to guide the reader.

While annotated bibliographies do not traditionally have chapter references, references are provided to support any critique or for further study; however, only references that point to material not already annotated within the chapter are listed to avoid repetition.

A final chapter summarises major findings regarding themes and provides suggestions for future research. Lastly, the researchers offer an appendix of the textbooks and pedagogical resources that emerged during the search, for use in the Canadian classroom.

This is an interpretive qualitative endeavour to produce an annotated bibliography that informs the research question: What is the history and development of PR scholarship in Canada? The result is a volume that chronologically captures much of that scholarship and those developments, with interpretation. Readers can become informed of the trajectory of scholarship, be apprised of the diverse nature of inquiry that has occurred and make their own observations and interpretations. Most importantly, they can identify gaps, gain inspiration and carve out research paths.

## Statement

This annotated bibliography is not exhaustive; however, it is quite extensive, capturing a great many sources. For example, while some French sources are included, it is acknowledged that some may have been missed due to translation limitations.

## References

CPRS. (2021, March). *PR profession: DEI study*. Léger Company. Report 82654–048. www.cprs.ca/About/News/2021-(1)/Canada%E2%80%99s-PR-industry-releases-first-comprehensive

Ferguson, S. D. (1993). *Public relations research and education: A survey of work done in Canada*. Unpublished paper presented to the annual meeting of the International Communication Association, Washington, DC.

Meyers, C. (2021). *Public relations history: Theory, practice, and profession*. Routledge.

Thurlow, A. (2015). A critical historiography of public relations in Canada: Rethinking an ahistorical symmetry. In *The Routledge companion to management and organizational history* (pp. 302–315). Routledge.

Thurlow, A., Kushniryk, A., Yue, A., Blotnicky, K., Cross, L., & Gonzales, F. (2014). *Report of the generally accepted practices (VIII) survey (Canadian)*. Mount Saint Vincent University. https://ec.msvu.ca/items/4e84d7ab-d567-4b90-96e0-38dfd62549d1

**Part Two**

# Annotated Bibliography

# 1 1930s to 1970s

- The earliest PR agency that can be ascertained was formed in 1929 by W. A. Lawrence of Montreal (Obituary: W. A. Lawrence, 1967).
- A form of PR scholarship in the Canadian context does not appear in the academic literature until Dickson (1933), who, as a government official of Ontario, examined public opinion of forest conservation. It is notable that this early article concerns itself with public opinion and with government as the theme of government-public communications will become prevalent in PR scholarship.
- Much of early scholarship and literature about PR in Canadian contexts appeared in non-communications journals. More discipline-specific journals only evolved later.
- CPRS was established in 1948, just one year after its U.S. counterpart, PRSA.
- Canadian practitioner Leonard Knott (1955) published what could be viewed as an early PR textbook; he shares advice derived from his professional experiences with clients from across many sectors of Canadian society including civil service, nonprofits and corporations.
- The year 1957 saw what was the first graduate thesis about PR in a Canadian context as Francis (1957) explored United States-Canada relations around the burgeoning energy industry in Alberta. Francis would become a leader in the industry (CPRS, 2024).
- The 1960s, while a period of growth in the industry, is noted as a 'silent decade' for its absence of any significant, or identifiable, scholarly or industry material. However, a fledgling PR program at Mount Royal College in Alberta was beginning to develop when, in the fall of 1969, a two-year PR vocational program was launched (Associate Diploma in Science – Communications Media and PR, housed within the Faculty of Arts and Sciences).
- The 1970s is the precursor to more formal study with the establishment of the *Canadian Journal of Communication* in 1974 as a potential research outlet. Additionally, PR research and more PR-specific scholars begin to develop.
- In 1977, Mount Saint Vincent University in Halifax launched the country's first four-year undergraduate degree program.

DOI: 10.4324/9781003507475-4

**Dickson, J. R. (1933). The development of public opinion in relation to forest reservation in Canada.** *Empire Forestry Journal*, *12* (2), 215–228.

Dickson analyses evolving public opinion around conservation and the forestry industry from 1872 to 1932, crediting federal agencies such as the Canadian Forestry Association and the Dominion Forestry service, among other federal groups, for leading the way in conservation efforts. Dickson notes public opinion methods and trends used such as "field lecture courses and other educational or propaganda work, such as the Junior Forest Warden movement" (p. 221–222). Many key players in the formation of public opinion about forestation in Canada are identified and the general nature of their public opinion efforts discussed. Such interest in public opinion, particularly by expansive organisations like the Empire Forestry Association, involved in forestation throughout the entire British Empire, is reflective of studies of the time concerning the influencing of public opinion with recognised works by public relations pioneer Edward Bernays (1923) and media critic Walter Lippmann (1922). Interestingly, Lippmann advocated for a larger role by governments in the steering of public opinion.

**Parker, W. E. (1942). [Review of book** *Public relations of public personnel agencies,* **by the Civil Service Assembly's Committee on Public Personnel Agencies of the United States and Canada. 1941].** *The Journal of Politics*, *4* (1), 124–126.

This review of the PR of civil service administrators points to the conscious development of PR functions in the civil sector in both the United States and Canada as early as 1941. Parker notes the effectiveness and relevance of the handbook both theoretically (with reference to two-way-street methods, for example) and practically. Parker highly recommends it as a valuable resource for any public service administrator. This work is indicative of the early development of PR in the civil sector and is evidence that the concept of two-way methods existed in the minds of both Canadian and U.S. civil service workers prior to the formalisation of the two-way symmetrical theoretical orientation of PR formalised by Grunig and Hunt (1984).

**Canadian Association for Adult Education. (1952).** *Let's tell people: Public relations for organizations.* **Canadian Association for Adult Education.**

Prepared for a consortium of nonprofit educational organisations, this is a collection of short articles (total of 36 pages) that provides guidance and advice for member organisations of the role and importance of PR to publicise their efforts and reach their audiences. Its contributors discuss PR as public service, the spoken word, journalism, films, broadcasting and publicity. The chapter contributors provide some clues as to some important historical figures in PR development in Canada. These warrant further investigation and include

J. Muir, president of RBC; John Heron, PR adviser of RBC; Stuart Richardson, PR assistant at Northern Electric Company and vice-president of CPRS; Beatrice Findlay, a director of CPRS and editor of its newsletter; Carl Dair, typographer; T. J. Allard, Canadian Association of Broadcasters; J. Rutherford, a Canadian newspaper editor; W. Arthur Irwin, commissioner of the National Film Board and former editor of *Maclean's* magazine.

**Knott, L. L. (1955). *The PR in profit: A guide to successful public relations in Canada*. McClelland & Stewart.**

This is an early and seminal work about PR in Canada written by a Canadian practitioner. Published in 1955, the writer of the preface thanks Knott for giving Canadians their own textbook, noting the paucity of information about PR in Canada except for some magazine articles. Included in Knott's book are many cases contemporary to the time period. They not only capture some of the PR development in Canada, they provide fodder for discussion. The book identifies certain personalities, companies, organisations and historical events of the time. Knott stresses that successful PR is dependent upon *relationships* and is more than publicity or creating some 'sizzle'. This idea of PR as *public relationships* would fade, however, with increased competition in the marketplace and lack of theoretical development of PR as a distinct profession. The idea would be resurrected academically, however, with the publication of Ferguson (1984, 2018) who drew attention to the *relationship* aspect of PR, opening new avenues of research. This book could be considered one of the earliest, if not the first, Canadian textbook about practice with a Canadian author and a collection of Canadian examples.

**Francis, J. (1957). *Public relations problems of American petroleum companies in Canada* [Master's Thesis, Boston University].**

This thesis is an examination of the growing oil industry in Alberta and PR problems surrounding it. Francis examines Canadian tensions in Alberta with the arrival of many U.S. petroleum firms and applies PR principles as potential solutions to the problem. The paper includes a history of United States-Canada relations, Canadian attitudes toward U.S. industry and Canadian concerns and complaints with regard to the petroleum industry.

The 1950s were the early days of the oil industry in Alberta, and Francis had a front row seat, capturing the sentiment of the time and applying his PR knowledge. John Francis is a central figure in the development of PR in Canada. Born in 1932 in Calgary, Alberta, he came of age when the Alberta economy was just becoming energy-based. He became a leader in his field as a president of CPRS and a principal in Francis, Williams and Johnson Ltd., a respected PR firm based in Western Canada. He is known as being the first Canadian to achieve a master's degree in PR (CPRS, 2024).

**Dawson, M. (1971).** *The Mountie from dime novel to Disney*. **Between The Lines**.

Historian Michael Dawson traces the changing representation of one of Canada's most ubiquitous symbols – the 'Mountie' of the Royal Canadian Mounted Police. Dawson examines defining moments in their history, explores depictions in media and critiques evolving narratives around the symbol. There is criticism of *revisionism* of the Mountie's public image away from historically less flattering aspects, and toward a more favourable progressive depiction. Dawson's work highlights the concepts of *symbol*, *myth*, *nationhood* and *community* in a Canadian context. The role and power of symbols in strategic communication has been a theme in PR scholarship; symbolic interactionism has been proposed as a theoretical origin for PR (Gordon, 1997; Braun, 2015). This work provides a Canadian context in which to explore impression management through symbol and myth.

**Singer, B. D. (1972).** *Communications in Canadian society*. **Copp Clark**.

This is an early communications textbook dedicated to the Canadian context, likely the first. It provided the basis of study for many PR students as programs began to emerge in Canada in the late '70s and onward. It has been through various iterations, authors and publishers and is now in its fifth edition (McKie & Singer, 2001).

**Wright, N. K. (1976). The challenge of public relations in Canada.** *Public Relations Quarterly*, *21* **(3), 23–25**.

In this short article, Wright outlines challenges within the PR in Canada. Anecdotally, Wright notes that Canadian audiences are somewhat more "low-key" in response to media, PR and advertising efforts (p. 23). Wright refers to the often-cited concept of Canada being more of a *mosaic* rather than a *melting pot* (in comparison to the United States) and builds upon the historical angst by Canadians to differentiate, and often distance, themselves from U.S. influence.

This article provides a foundational reading by which to understand some of the Canadian culture and mentality. Wright alludes to the francophone community in Canada, the country's multiculturalism and the efforts by governments to identify, maintain and promote that which is deemed to be *Canadian*, all in search of a seemingly elusive identity. Wright taps into this angst. The notion of Canadian identity has been an ongoing topic of discussion by the Canadian general public and also by historians. Deeper understanding of these questions can be understood by some of the classic works of Canadian historian Pierre Berton (1975, 1982), and exploration in the PR context can contribute to the development of distinct PR narratives in the Canadian context.

**Ontario Editorial Bureau.** (1976) *Public relations in the making: A review of significant events in Canadian communication.* Archives & Special Collections, Brock University.

This is a booklet of selected PR projects by the Ontario Editorial Bureau, an early PR agency. The author, presumably founder Lou Cahill, traces work for clients from 1947–1975 such as the Niagara Falls Commission, Canadian Centennial, Duke of Edinburgh's Study Conference, Canadian Census and Canada Savings Bonds, among others. This is an excellent snapshot of early modern practice in Canada.

**Stanley, G. F. (1978). The man who made Canada: 1865–1867.** *Public Relations Review* , *4* (3), 38–51.

In recognition of the founding of Canada's Confederation, a Canadian historian and author addresses the conference of the PRSA on November 9, 1964, in Montreal. Stanley highlights the person and work of John A. MacDonald, Canada's first prime minister, for his "intuitive understanding of public relations" (p. 4). Stanley challenges the PR practitioners gathered in Montreal to view the work of MacDonald's Confederation-building work as a template for the exercise of masterful PR in the ongoing promotion of Canadian unity.

## References

Bernays, E. L. (1923). *Crystallizing public opinion.* Boni and Liveright.

Berton, P. (1975). *Hollywood's Canada: The Americanization of our national image.* McClelland and Stewart.

Berton, P. (1982). *Why we act like Canadians: A personal exploration of our national character.* McClelland and Stewart.

Braun, S. (2015). Can we all agree? Building the case for symbolic interactionism as the theoretical origins of public relations. *Journal of Professional Communication, 4*(1), 49–70.

CPRS. (2024). *John Francis.* www.cprs.ca/About/Yocom-Public-Relations-Profiles/John-Francis?lang=fr-CA

Ferguson, M. A. (1984, August). *Building theory in public relations: Interorganizational relationships* [Conference presentation]. Annual meeting of the association for education in journalism and mass communication, Gainesville, FL.

Ferguson, M. A. (2018). Building theory in public relations: Interorganizational relationships as a public relations paradigm. *Journal of Public Relations Research, 30*(4), 164–178.

Gordon, J. C. (1997). Interpreting definitions of public relations: Self assessment and a symbolic interactionism-based alternative. *Public Relations Review, 23*(1), 57–66.

Grunig, J. E., & Hunt, T. (1984). *Managing public relations.* Holt, Rinehart and Winston.

Lippmann, W. (1922). *Public opinion*. Harcourt, Brace and Company.

McKie, C., & Singer, B. D. (2001). *Communications in Canadian society* (5th ed.). Thompson.

Obituary: W. A. Lawrence. (1967, July 19). *Montreal Star*, p. 62 [Microfilm Image].

# 2 1980s

- The 1980s saw the development of the foundations of a consistent body of knowledge of modern PR scholarship in the Canadian context. Interest in the topic of public opinion remained, and another possibility for a textbook emerged (Herbert & Jenkins, 1984).
- The earliest published PR studies in the Canadian context were set against the backdrop of the feminist movement. An early scholar, Judith Scrimger (1985), is noted as a PR-specific scholar with an early publication about Canadian practice in a public relations–dedicated journal, *Public Relations Review*, sharing a study about Canadian women in PR. This is likely the first piece of empirical research about a PR topic in the Canadian context published in a PR academic journal. Additionally, late in the decade, Piekos and Einsiedel (1989), graduate students of the program of communications studies at University of Calgary, made a conference presentation of their quantitative study documenting the experience of women in practice in Canada.

**Young, W. R. (1981a). Building citizenship: English Canada and propaganda during the Second War. *Journal of Canadian Studies, 16* (3–4), 121–132.**

Young examines propagandist messages by Canada's Bureau of Public Information, Canada's first propaganda agency. The Bureau, similar to its U.S. counterpart, the Creel Committee, rallied the nation around pro-war sentiment. Young examines some of this messaging from the early days of beckoning Canadians toward a common goal, to the 1939–1942 messaging around *Canadianism* and the promotion of shared experiences as ways to unify public sentiment. The Bureau became the Wartime Information Board in 1942; it remained active in building consensus around other issues such as the development of participatory citizenship. The Board was eventually co-opted by the Liberal Party in 1945, and any notions the Board had of building a more democratic citizenry became lost to political ends. Propagandist messaging during times of war, particularly in Canada's early history, have not been as extensively studied as the United States. A comparison of messaging between

DOI: 10.4324/9781003507475-5

the two nations to show similarities, and differences, can likely help distinguish any peculiarities or particularities in the Canadian mindset.

**Young, W. R. (1981b). A highly intelligent and unselfish approach: Public information and the Canadian West: 1939–1945.** *Canadian Historical Review*, *62*, 496–520.

Young continues his discussion of the Wartime Information Board, this time in the context of perceived resistance for wartime activities by the West. Surveys at the time, however, showed good support by the West with a greater propensity for wartime sacrifice than had been supposed. The Canadian cultural and political landscape has long been dominated by East-West differentiations and sometimes division. Studies that compare and contrast the two regions could provide the basis upon which PR theory, such as two-way symmetrical approaches, could be tested or enacted in the Canadian context.

**Taylor, S. M., Hall, G. B., Hughes, R. C., & Dear, M. J. (1984). Predicting community reaction to mental health facilities.** *Journal of the American Planning Association*, *50* (1), 36–47.

This empirical study, conducted in Toronto, tests a model to predict neighbourhood responses to community-based mental healthcare facilities. Rate of transience levels within the community, scarcity of children in households and economic status were concluded to be predictors of attitudes towards facilities. Another key finding was that neighbourhood reaction to facilities became increasingly negative as distance from the city centre increased, leading researchers to conclude that metropolitan centres provided the best option for the location of facilities.

**Herbert, W. B., & Jenkins, R. G. (1984).** *Public relations in Canada: Some perspectives*. **Fitzhenry & Whiteside Limited.**

This edited collection of 57 essays documents the perspectives of 42 leading PR practitioners of the time. This book was commissioned through a grant by CPRS as a textbook for emerging practitioners. With a dearth of literature available about Canada's PR past, this work leaves many breadcrumbs for historians to gather and investigate.

**Scrimger, J. (1985). Profile: Women in Canadian PR.** *Public Relations Review*, *11* (3), 40–46.

This empirical study examines women in the field in Canada through a questionnaire of 186 female practitioners. The findings demonstrate that the majority of female practitioners were middle level management with few holding senior management titles. Significant job and salary satisfaction was also documented. Scrimger pressed for greater education for women in order to access higher positions in firms. Scrimger highly encouraged further education since more than 50% of the sample in the study did not hold university degrees. Additionally, gender discrimination issues were raised by many practitioners.

**Groome, M. E. (1987).** *Canada's Stratford Festival 1953–1967: Hegemony, commodity, institution* **[Doctoral Dissertation, McGill University]**.

This is a critical cultural analysis of promotional materials of Canada's popular Stratford Festival, 1953–1967. Statements of the institutional discourse were identified and analysed. The researcher argues that the discourse was largely hegemonic and criticises the event for being part of the mass culture industry as purported by Horkheimer and Adorno (1947). PR and the arts is an avenue that has not been widely explored. This represents an early example of study.

**Lorimer, R., & McNulty, J. (1987).** *Mass communication in Canada.* **McClelland and Stewart**.

This early mass communication textbook is focused on the Canadian context and has evolved to its ninth edition (Lorimer et al., 2017; Gasher et al., 2020).

**Piekos, J. M., & Einsiedel, E. F. (1989, August 10–13).** *Gender and decision-making among Canadian public relations practitioners* **[Conference Session]. Public Relations Division, AEJMC. Washington, DC**.

A study of about 300 survey respondents from metropolitan centres in Canada revealed that a) women in PR tended to earn less than their male counterparts; b) salaries appeared to be based on years of experience; c) there were no differences between gender and decision-making approaches (whether intuitive versus scientific); d) women in higher roles participated in policy decisions just as often as men; and e) 47% said they perceived the influence of women on the profession as positive. Some aspects of this study were contrary to U.S. findings; for example, U.S. studies suggested a strong gender divide between roles, particularly in managerial positions.

This study is representative of the times with the establishment of the second wave of feminism (see Cline et al., 1986) and follows Scrimger (1985).

**Shiller, Ed. (1989).** *Managing the media.* **Bedford House**.

Shiller's guide to media management provides an undergraduate-level primer on media relations that is relevant today. As a public relations executive and also instructor on the topic, Shiller writes in accessible style  about the basics of newsworthiness, knowing your organisation, credibility, planning a media relations program, compiling lists and interviewing. While the focus is on mass media, the basic tenets of media relations are strong and well-explained in this volume.

Later editions (1993; 1994) were re-named *The Canadian Guide to Managing the Media* and included chapters on crisis communication. Extensive case studies in the 1994 volume include Amoco Canada's proposed merger with Dome Petroleum; image enhancement of Quintette Coal Ltd. in British Columbia; the Canadian Manufacturers' Association's response to the 1986 Throne Speech; celebrating the blessing of the bells of the Slovak Cathedral of the Transfiguration following a papal visit; and the promotion of an invention by a local chiropractor. Each case study guides students through the steps and the news releases written for each media campaign.

**Vipond, M. (1989). *The mass media in Canada* (1st ed.). James Lorimer & Company, Ltd.**

Vipond, a professor emeritus of history at Concordia University in Montreal and a president of the Canadian Historical Society (2003–2004), produced one of the early textbooks about mass media in Canada, a foundational topic to the study of PR. Some programs of PR had already been established in Canada by this time, and this textbook provided communications students with a relevant resource. This book is now in its fourth edition (Vipond, 2011).

## References

Cline, C., Toth, E., Turk, J., Walters, L., Johnson, N., & Smith, H. (1986). *The velvet ghetto: The impact of the increasing percentage of women in public relations and business communication*. USA, IABC Foundation.

Gasher, M., Skinner, D., & Coulter, N. (2020). *Media and communication in Canada: Networks, culture, technology, audiences* (9th ed.). Oxford University Press.

Horkheimer, M., & Adorno, T. W. (1947). *Dialektik der Aufklärung*. Querido.

Lorimer, R., Gasher, M., & Skinner, D. (2017). *Mass communication in Canada* (8th ed.). Langara College.

Shiller, Ed. (1994). *The Canadian guide to managing the media* (Revised ed.). Prentice Hall.

Vipond, M. (2011). *Mass media in Canada* (4th ed.). James Lorimer & Company, Ltd.

# 3    1990s

- In this decade, an early Canadian study appears in a public relations journal with a study by Piekos and Einsiedel (1990).
- An introductory work of history of public relations research in Canada was captured with Ferguson (1993) in an unpublished paper, which was not retrievable for reference.
- Emms (1995) produced a seminal thesis documenting the emergence and evolution of modern practice in Canada.
- Works around crisis management emerge.
- Research around issues related to the environment and activism emerges.

**Piekos, J., & Einsiedel, E. (1990). Roles and program evaluation techniques among Canadian public relation practitioners. In L. A. Grunig & J. E. Grunig (Eds.), *Public Relations Research Annual: Vol. 2* (pp. 95–113). Routledge.**

This article analyses the extent to which program evaluation was prevalent in public relations departments across Canada. The researchers found that intuitive methods of evaluation were more common than scientific ones, and Canadian communications technicians differed from those in U.S. contexts in that Canadians used program evaluations more frequently. Researchers noted a positive association between managerial roles and the use of formal program evaluation, encouraging practitioners to receive training and knowledge in formal evaluation methods.

**Trent, B. (1991). Psychiatrists confront an image problem. *Canadian Medical Association Journal, 144* (12), 1651–1655.**

The Canadian Psychiatric Association enlisted public relations and marketing professionals to research the problem of concerns around stigma around mental health and negative public image of the profession. Researchers identified some of the issues as a) psychiatrists' own avoidance of media; b) low public profile; c) an ill-defined public image; d) unwillingness to use advancing technology; and e) failure to communicate success stories. This is one of a few detailed case studies in the Canadian context from this time period.

DOI: 10.4324/9781003507475-6

**Hoggan, J. (1991). Open door public relations: A new strategy for the 1990s.** *Business Quarterly, 56* (2), 22.

This commentary identifies *media criticism* as a reason for lack of public enthusiasm toward large corporations. Hoggan challenges corporations to eschew practices like media avoidance and urges *open door public relations* for image repair. Hoggan provides guidance in the construction of more transparent corporate messages.

**Ferguson, S. D. (1993).** *Public relations research and education: A survey of work done in Canada.* **Unpublished paper presented to the Annual Meeting of the International Communication Association, Washington, DC.**

While the contents of this paper appear to be lost to history, it is notable that this line of research was opened.

**Johnston, C. (1993). Researchers, animal rights activists fight public relations war at Western.** *Canadian Medical Association Journal, 148* (8), 1349–1353.

This article explores the influence of animal right activism on medical research ethics, particularly noting controversial experiments being conducted on baboons and monkeys at the University of Western Ontario. Johnston urges medical personnel toward awareness that research is open to public scrutiny, thus making it a public relations concern. Johnston notes growing sensitivities in the society around ethics and medical practices, warning researchers to take the concerns of activists seriously and to understand their power and influence.

At this time, public relations as activism was just being hinted at in the public relations literature but would become more popular, particularly through the later work of Holtzhausen (2000) who discussed postmodern values in public relations and advocated for activism as a postmodernism expression of public relations.

**Donoghue, J. (1993).** *PR: Fifty years in the field.* **Dundurn Press.**

This memoir details the career of public relations professional Jack Donoghue (1916–2001) across five decades in communications in the military, public and private sectors. There are references to certain historical events including Manitoba's 1950 flood, the 1953 polio epidemic, some early history of public relations in Canada's public sector, the Canada Water Act, the Alberta nurse's strike of 1977, the struggle between the Independent Petroleum Association of Canada and the federal government and other events.

The lives of Canadian public relations influencers and leaders have not been well documented. Brief biographies can be found in various documents and on the CPRS website; however, many figures have been missed, and treatments are basic. There is much opportunity for research in this area. This is one of the few formal autobiographies or biographies of a Canadian public relations leader.

**Parker, E. (1993).** *I didn't come here to stay: The memoirs of Ed Parker.* **Natural Heritage/Natural History Inc**.

Ed Parker (1918–1988) was a journalist and public relations practitioner who founded the School of Journalism and Graphic Arts in Toronto. This memoir takes readers through Parker's early days in Winnipeg and highlights efforts during the uranium boom of the 1950s. This work is one of the few detailed treatments of a Canadian PR figure.

**Dodds, D., & Swinairski, D. (1994).** *The first 120 minutes: A guide to crisis management in education.* **Canadian Education Association**.

This work is a guide to effective crisis management prepared for educators and educational institutions. It focuses on best practices at Johnson & Johnson, Wisconsin Electric Power Company and Molson Breweries. The authors discuss catastrophic crises and point to the first 120 minutes of a crisis as being the most critical in public opinion formation. It includes reflection and self-assessment exercises. Crisis management studies will increase in the coming decades and become a popular topic of study.

**Marsden, M. T. (1994). The Royal Bank of Canada's** *Letter* **as international educational tool.** *Journal of American Culture, 17* **(4), 41–45**.

Marsden examines RBC's monthly newsletter as a tool of international education to promote Canadian life and culture to customers and audiences around the world. While Marsden does not use the term *public relations* (only noting that the editor of the newsletter was a *public relations person*), he calls the publication a powerful "international tool for planting positive perspectives" (p. 45).

This is an early Canada-specific article that provides some foundational knowledge of an influential print publication by a major Canadian institution. RBC exists today and is an icon of Canadian banking and finance.

**Emms, M. J. (1995).** *The origins of public relations as an occupation in Canada* **[Master's Thesis, Concordia University, Montreal]**.

A seminal work, Emms' thesis explores the origins of public relations in Canada, citing the immigration campaign by the Canadian Pacific Railway of the late nineteenth century as a likely starting point of modern practice. Using available documents from corporate and national archives, Emms explores other contexts in which the public relations function can be identified, such as work within the department of agriculture through J. A. Donaldson in 1893, who was possibly Canada's first government publicist; immigration efforts to attract settlers from Britain, particularly under the direction of Sir Charles Tupper; work done by the department of the interior; efforts by Bell Telephone Company to sway public opinion away from government-owned telephone businesses; and early public relations development within RBC. The study includes interviews with four Canadian practitioners: Munro Brown, who worked at the Bank of Montreal (circa 1932); Lou Cahill of Ontario Editorial Bureau, whose public relations work commenced in the 1930s; Jack Donoghue, who began in military public relations during WWII; and Ruth Hammond, whose public relations career began in the 1950s.

This is likely the first comprehensive exploration about the history of public relations development in Canada and is a seminal work. It contains many insights and references and provides many historical threads to unravel.

**Hacker, D. (1995).** *A Canadian's writer's reference.* **Nelson Thomson Learning.**

Canadian college students had been traditionally relying upon U.S.-based writing handbooks; however, with the inception of Hacker's Canadian reference, students would now have access to localised word usage and spelling. This writing handbook has been beneficial for Canadian post-secondary students across many disciplines including public relations and journalism. The work remains in publication today as Hacker and Sommers (2021).

**Hewitt, M. (1995). The itinerant emigration lecturer: James Brown's lecture tour of Britain and Ireland, 1861–1862.** *British Journal of Canadian Studies, 10* **(1), 103–119.**

Hewitt traces the promotional activities of Surveyor General James Brown of New Brunswick to attract immigrants in the pre-Dominion of Canada period. Promotional activities were re-constructed and analysed based on Brown's diaries, correspondence and reports. In addition to newspaper advertisements and posters, emigration lecturers like Brown provided points of personal contact to potential immigrants. Brown was able to provide valuable general information; however, his inability to provide practical support, like booking overseas passage, hindered efforts. In spite of this, Brown's work provided the groundwork for subsequent later successful recruitment efforts, specifically by A. C. Buchanan, who added the element of a residential agency to facilitate a more successful emigration process. This work fills a gap in the literature of public relations history in Canada by describing the communications and recruitment activities of such agents.

Lorimer, R., & McNulty, J. (1996). *Mass communication in Canada* (3rd ed.). Oxford University Press.

A popular textbook among communications students, it is in its eighth edition (Lorimer et al., 2017).

Putnam, K. G. (1997). *The origins and history of the first public relations consultancy to operate in Toronto.* Ryerson Polytechnic Institute.

This paper is believed to be unpublished as it cannot be located, and attempts to retrieve it have been unsuccessful.

Sherman, J., & Gismondi, M. (1997). Jock talk, goldfish, horse logging and Star Wars. *Alternatives Journal, 23* (1), 14–20.

Researchers examined public relations techniques used by Alpac, an Alberta-based pulp mill, to manage its public image in the face of growing public criticism of pulp and logging practices. To counter negative sentiment, Alpac marketers and communicators created a newsletter, *Forest Landscape*, which was quite successful. Through a content analysis of the publication, the researchers wished to identify the communications techniques employed within the newsletter that likely contributed to the reversal. They identified a) positively-framed headlines; b) careful framing of issues; c) capitalising on 'warm and fuzzy' imagery; d) an emphasis on technology and advancement as part of key messaging; and e) the labelling of environmentalists as 'extremists'.

This article captures the Canadian consciousness with respect to the environment. This study also hints at the history of communications by the forestry industry; organisations built around natural resources were among some of the first to embrace research into public opinion research, public relations and strategic communication. (See Dickson, 1933.). This article is also testament to the fact that studies in strategic communication and public relations in the Canadian context were being done, but not always by communications researchers and not appearing in the *Canadian Journal of Communication*, established in 1974. (Such articles do not appear in the journal until about 2009.)

Lachanche, P. (1997). The new power of NGOs as viewed from Canada [Monograph]. In *Worldview focus: The new power of non-governmental organizations* (pp. 7–10). Adaptation of a presentation to the XIV IPRA Public Relations World Congress of June 16, 1997. Public Relations Society of America.

Pierre Lachance, principal of Optimum Public Relations in Montreal, reflected on the growing influence of NGOs to facilitate dialogue between industry and government. He noted the important process of public consultation as emerging in the 1990s in contrast to avoidance strategies of the 1980s. LaChance called for the public relations profession to include *issue scanning* and *analysis* in communications programs to identify emerging issues and publics. He pointed to the case of Alcan Aluminum Ltd., the first industrial project to be subjected to Canada's new environmental impact study laws, as a success story.

**Cobban, W. (Director) (1998).** *Mountie: Canada's mightiest myth* **[Film]. National Film Board of Canada**.

Film, TV clips and archival news footage are used to examine the myth of the Canadian 'Mountie', illustrating the reductionism of mass media images. Figures such as Nelson Eddy, Sergeant Preston, Dudley Do-Right and Canadian actor Paul Gross are all pictured and discussed.

PR explorations into the current status of the country's image abroad in terms of myths and symbols are warranted in light of ever-shifting global politics.

**Grunig, L. A., Grunig, J. E., & Vercic, D. (1998). Are the IABC's excellence principles generic? Comparing Slovenia and the United States, the United Kingdom and Canada.** *Journal of Communication Management,* **2 (4), 335–356**.

This article assesses some principles of successful public relations identified by the IABC *Excellence Study*, comparing Slovenia against the United Kingdom, United States and Canada through a survey of 300 organisations. All countries showed strong correlations, with Slovenia exhibiting slightly lower scores in terms of *strategic management* and *public relations being valued by upper management*. CEOs in Canada valued the public relations department less than their counterparts in the United States and the United Kingdom. Similarly, the *two-way symmetrical* and *asymmetrical* models were reported to be less preferred amongst Canadian communicators than those in the United Kingdom, by comparison.

　　This is an extensive study of which results were published across many papers and books and is deserving of examination to situate Canadian practice.

**Warsame, H., Pedwell, K., & Neu, D. (1998). Managing public impressions: Environmental disclosures in annual reports.** *Accounting, Organizations and Society,* **23 (3), 265–282**.

Researchers examine the use of CSR environmental disclosures by companies to garner public favour and claim social legitimacy. The researchers use content analysis of the annual reports of 33 organisations involved in oil, gas, mineral extraction, forestry and chemicals during the period 1982–1991. They discovered that the level of disclosure was associated with a) the levels of shareholder concerns; b) the degree of criticism by environmental groups; and c) the level of societal attention. Large companies tended to disclose more than smaller ones.

**Maisonneuve, D., Lamarche, J.-F., et St-Amand, Y. (1998).** *Les relations publiques dans une société en mouvance* **(1e éd.). PUQ.**

This French PR textbook (translated as *Public Relations in a Changing Society*) is an excellent reference work for francophone students, winning the Price Waterhouse Cooper's Business Book Prize. It includes the *Code of Ethics of the Québec Society of Public Relations Professionals* and the *Declaration of Québec Communicators and Public Relations Professionals Regarding Sustainable Development* as well as Québec case studies. Later editions added chapters on evaluation and measurement and ethics. (See Maisonneuve, 2010.)

## References

Dickson, J. R. (1933). The development of public opinion in relation to forest reservation in Canada. *Empire Forestry Journal, 12*(2), 215–228.

Hacker, D., & Sommers, N. (2021). *A Canadian writer's reference* (7th ed.). Bedford St. Martin's.

Holtzhausen, D. R. (2000). Postmodern values in public relations. *Journal of Public Relations Research, 12*(1), 93–114.

Lorimer, R., Gasher, M., & Skinner, D. (2017). *Mass communication in Canada* (8th ed.). Langara College.

Maisonneuve, D. (2010). *Les relations publiques dans une société en mouvance* (4e éd.). PUQ.

# 4 2000s

- This is the decade of the laying of important groundwork. PR research in Canadian contexts begins to sprout. While sporadic articles continue to appear in journals across varying domains such as *Journal of Hazardous Materials*, *Sociological Quarterly* and *Journal of Management Studies*, more articles begin to appear in communications journals such as *Journal of Communication Management* (a publication by the European Public Relations Education and Research Association), *Public Relations Research* and *Public Relations Review*. Topics and the approaches remain varied.
- In 2008, a Canadian definition of PR was put forward, which was an important development in the discipline.
- Canadian-based communications journals, like the *Canadian Journal of Communication*, began to publish more Canadian content near the end of the decade.
- There was a surge of relevant textbooks during this decade, with nine publications.
- This decade saw the beginnings of the rise of social media. In 2009, an early examination of PR and social media in a Canadian context appeared in *Global Media Journal*. Researchers studied the digital media presence of environmental nonprofit organisations in Canada.
- There was an injection of PR in the Canadian context appearing in the *McMaster Journal of Communication* (out of McMaster University) in 2009, particularly with the special edition of Volume 6(1) entitled *Strategic Communication*. This interdisciplinary journal was formed in 2004 to showcase excellent student work. With the launch of the Communication and New Media graduate program in 2009 and the addition of the McMaster-Syracuse Master of Communications Management program in 2011, a sister publication to the earlier journal, *Journal of Professional Communication*, would also follow in 2010. This publication would invite academic, student and industry-based researchers. These two publications would become the primary vehicles showcasing PR research in the Canadian context, and by the end of the decade, some foundations for the acceleration of scholarship began to develop, laying the groundwork for a surge of scholarship in the coming decade.

DOI: 10.4324/9781003507475-7

Davies, E. (2000). Canada's public relations response to the myth of violence: The 1995 Firearms Act [Bill C-68]. [Winner 2000 Cassels Brock & Blackwell Paper Prize]. *Appeal Review of Current Law and Law Reform, 6* (1), 44–59.

A law student analyses the 1995 Firearms Act and amendments to the *Criminal Code of Canada*, which generated much controversy. The researcher concludes that the enactment of the legislation drew inordinate attention to the matter, causing Canadians to believe that the level of violence in the society had been increasing when, in fact, survey showed it had been decreasing. The researcher concludes that the Act created more publicity issues than it solved.

Kugler, M. (2000). *Des campagnes de communication réussies tome 2.* Les Presses de l'Université du Québec.

Kugler examines Canadian PR campaigns from 2003–2007, applying relevant theories. Cases from across the spectrum of public health, product launches and crisis management are examined. This is a useful textbook for students of PR in the francophone context and has been published in many editions. (See Kugler, 2010.)

Schoening-Thiessen, K., & Conference Board of Canada. (2000). *Ambassadors of goodwill: Key insights of some well-known case studies in risk and crisis communication (Ser. Case Studies, 290–00).* Conference Board of Canada.

This collection of case studies emphasises the importance of creating goodwill between stakeholders and companies during times of risk. Best practices are outlined. Cases include Sterling Pulp Chemicals' expansion into the southeastern United States; Hydro-Québec in the 1998 ice storm crisis; Canadian Blood Services; and the City of Hamilton's environmental performance plan.

Denis, H. (2001). Managing disasters involving hazardous substances in Canada: Technical and sociopolitical issues. *Journal of Hazardous Materials, 88* (2), 195–211.

Denis examines four case studies of disasters in Québec from 1988–1985 from the viewpoints of *complexity* and *uncertainty*. They are examined in the context of *technical* variables (e.g., safety, search-and-rescue) and *socio-political* variables (e.g., evacuation and medical care). Highlighting public health and environmental concerns, the author argues for mandatory reporting by companies and local governments to calm the uncertainty between socio-political concerns and technical management during crises.

**Johansen, P. (2001). Professionalisation, building respectability, and the birth of the Canadian Public Relations Society.** *Journalism Studies, 2* **(1), 55–71.**

Johansen traces the early development of the CPRS through the lens of *professionalisation.* There is some discussion of PR historical development in Canada in the post-WWII years.

The researcher judges PR in Canada to be *semi-professional* and recommends mandatory licensing as a tool to enhance professionalisation.

**Attallah, P. M., & Shade, L. R. (2002).** *Mediascapes: New patterns in Canadian communication.* **Nelson Thomson.**

This is an overview of mass communication in Canada, covering radio, film, recording, television, Aboriginal issues, convergence, copyright, online journalism, internet and socio-cultural issues, among others. It is now in its fourth edition (Shade, 2014). The newest edition includes discussions of social media, privacy and diversity.

**Carney, W. W. (2002).** *In the news: The practice of media relations in Canada.* **University of Alberta Press.**

Aimed as a textbook for university students of media studies and communications, this book fills the gap in the literature for a broad-based summary of media relations practice in Canada, addressing both theory and practice. It is now in its third edition (Carney et al., 2019).

**Communication Canada. (2002).** *Public opinion research in the government of Canada: An orientation guide.* **Communication Canada.**

This guide was created for departments within the Government of Canada to increase their understanding of public opinion research. It describes the department's data collection methods and practices.

**Dufour, G., & National Public Relations Inc. (2002).** *National: 25 years of public relations.* **National Public Relations.**

National Public Relations holds a unique place in the history of PR in Canada. Created in Montreal in 1976 by Luc Beauregard, it is often touted as Canada's largest PR operation. Some examination of its archive could add to the literature about PR history.

**Empry, G. (2002).** *I belong to the stars: Adventures in public relations.* **Mosaic Press.**

Toronto-born entertainment promoter Gino Empry (1925–2006) was well known in the Canadian entertainment scene as a promoter of many famous

Canadian entertainers such as Anne Murray, Celine Dion, the Irish Rovers and Gordon Pinsent, among others. Empry opened his entertainment agency in 1964. Many students are interested in entertainment PR. Works such as this provide some history to the specialty.

**Grunig, J. E., & Grunig, L. A. (2002). The implications of the IABC Excellence Study for PR education.** *Journal of Communication Management,* **7 (1), 34–42**.

This article summarises the main implications of the 15-year IABC *Excellence Study* with regard to PR education, concluding that students must learn that a) PR is a strategic communications function within organisations; b) PR education at the graduate level should focus on strategic management and research skills; c) ethics should be studied in the context of PR practice; and d) PR should be studied and viewed as a global profession. This study is significant in that it included three countries: Canada, the United States and the United Kingdom. See following for results in relation to Canada.

**Grunig, J. E., Dozier, D. M., & Grunig, J. E. (2002).** *Excellent public relations and effective organizations: A study of communication management in three countries* **(1st ed.). Routledge**.

This book is based on the 15-year IABC *Excellence Study* to identify the significance and value of the PR function to organisations. With respect to country comparisons, Canada showed slightly more female communications department heads (61%) than the United States (51%) or the United Kingdom (40%). Canada had a significantly higher preference of the three countries for the *two-way symmetrical* model; scored highest in strategic planning; had PR heads in the media relations/advisors/manager roles; was most likely to have a communications head in the dominant coalition; exhibited a participative culture; and its CEOs tended to value the PR function least among the three nations. There were no significant differences between the three countries in terms of adherence to factors deemed to be *excellent* as explicated in *Excellence Theory*. The book contains detailed quantitative and qualitative data and would be of interest to applied researchers, scholars and students.

**Guiniven, J. E. (2002). Dealing with activism in Canada: An ideal cultural fit for the two-way symmetrical public relations model.** *Public Relations Review,* **28 (4), 393–402**.

Guiniven determines that those who work in activism in the United States and Canada deal with issues differently in terms of level of confrontation. Guiniven argues that this difference is likely rooted in a tradition of compromise in Canadian culture. Through a series of 15 in-depth interviews, the researcher discusses models of PR and suggests that the *two-way sym-metrical* model based on Grunig and Hunt (1984) is a cultural fit for Cana-dian PR.

Other researchers have noted the likely connection between *two-way sym-metry* and the Canadian psyche (see Johansen, 2001; Grunig et al., 2002). This is deserving of more research utilising empirical methods.

**Sinclair, A. J. (2002). Public consultation for sustainable development policy initiatives: Manitoba approaches.** *Policy Studies Journal, 30* **(4), 423–443.**

This article analyses sustainable policy development in Canada, arguing that early and more fulsome public consultation at the planning level of policy-making by government and organisations would produce more effec-tive results. The researcher uses a case study of sustainable development legislation in Manitoba as an example of effective consultation and suggests techniques such as *education* and *participatory opportunities* could accelerate policy and innovations.

*Public consultation* as a unit of analysis to examine *two-way symmetry* could prove to be an informative and beneficial set of studies in the Canadian context.

**Sommers, S. (2002).** *Building media relationships: How to establish, main-tain and develop long-term relationships with the media.* **Irwin.**

Sommers' book is a guide to understanding and practice of media relations, suitable for students and available in a second edition (Sommers, 2009).

**Dewhirst, T., & Sparks, R. (2003). Intertextuality, tobacco sponsorship of sports, and adolescent male smoking culture: A selective review of tobacco industry documents.** *Journal of Sport & Social Issues, 27* **(4), 372–398.**

Researchers explore evidence that suggests Canadian tobacco brands Play-ers, Export A and Dunhill targeted male adolescents through commissioned research and sport sponsorship strategies.

**Fleras, A. (2003).** *Mass media communication in Canada.* **Top Hat.**

Written for the Canadian context, Fleras offers a critical cultural per-spective examining media as a power centre. Case studies are provided to facilitate examination of issues that lie at the intersection of media and Canadian society (e.g., gender, multiculturalism, minorities and nation-building). Marshall McLuhan, Canadian philosopher and media theorist, is referenced.

**Hallahan, K. (2003). W.L. Mackenzie King: Rockefeller's 'other' public relations counsellor in Colorado. *Public Relations Review*, *29* (4), 401–414.**

Hallahan argues that William Lyon Mackenzie King's (the tenth prime minister of Canada) role in the legacy and history of PR is greater than previously considered as King was a counsellor to John D. Rockefeller Jr. during the historical Colorado coal strike and Ludlow Massacre of 1913–1914. King's views, interestingly, also included a coherent communication approach that resembles what is now termed the *two-way symmetrical model* (Grunig & Hunt, 1984; Coatney, 2012).

**Potter, E. (2003). Canada and the new public diplomacy. *International Journal*, *58* (1), 43–64.**

Potter asserts that Canada has many strengths to showcase on the world stage and is not fulsomely exerting its potential. Potter urges Canada to become more proactive in identifying controversial global issues, asserting itself on the global arena and utilising all its tools of soft power to become a more effective world power.

   This work taps into an aspect of Canada's national character sometimes identified as 'passive', 'polite' or 'low-key' or their equivalents. This characteristic is an interesting feature often assigned to the Canadian psyche, which is worthy of study from a PR perspective. (See Wright, 1976.)

**Scrimger, J., & Richards, T. (2003). Public relations battles and wars: Journalistic clichés and the potential for conflict resolution. *Public Relations Review*, *29* (4), 485–492.**

Scrimger and Richards examined 63 newspaper articles for journalists' use of the term *battle* or *war* to describe a PR situation. The researchers challenged journalists to pursue a more factual and accurate depiction of PR situations rather than rely on overly broad journalistic interpretation or oversimplification.

**Detre, L. A. (2004). Canada's campaign for immigrants and the images in *Canada West* magazine. *Great Plains Quarterly*, *24* (2), 113–129.**

Detre analyses magazine covers to illustrate intentional and systematic efforts by the Canadian government to attract primarily British immigrants to the prairie provinces of Saskatchewan, Alberta and Manitoba.

**Kugler, M. (2004). *Des campagnes de communication réussies. 43 études de cas primés*. Presses de l'Université du Québec.**

Kugler systematically reviewed 43 award-winning campaigns from 1988–2001 utilising three complementary models. Designed as a textbook, this provides francophone students of PR with a scientifically based method of PR case analysis.

**Baumann, B. A. (2005).** *Bonjour Canada: A case study of the 1995–2000 Louisiana public relations campaign to attract Canadian visitors to Louisiana* **[Doctoral thesis, Louisiana State University]**.

Baumann's doctoral thesis is a case study of the PR techniques used by the state of Louisiana to encourage tourism from Canada. A *two-way asymmetric* model was used to target the French-speaking demographic of Canada. Key messages appealing to their common French Cajun heritage were used. Organisers felt the campaign was a success, while some in the Louisiana Cajun community felt the way in which they were depicted in the Canadian campaign perpetuated stereotypes.

Canada's French-English duality provides an area of rich study for PR practice and theory against evolving PR theoretical frameworks. Additionally, historical French-English tensions could benefit by nuanced examination through a PR lens utilising theoretical frameworks from the discipline such as *two-way symmetry* or *contingency theory of accommodation* or *Balance Zone Theory* or even new approaches. (See Grunig & Hunt, 1984; Cancel et al., 1997; Flynn, 2006.)

**Flynn, T. T. (2005).** *Organizational crisis public relations management in Canada and the United States: Constructing a predictive model of crisis preparedness* **[Doctoral thesis, Syracuse University]. ProQuest**.

Flynn's dissertation is a key quantitative study of PR crisis management in Canada and the United States to test a predictive model of *crisis preparedness*. In an analysis of 468 PR officers, this study examined the contribution of six independent variables on an organisation's crisis preparedness, utilising the survey method. The researcher determined that the resulting *Organisational Crisis Public Relations Management Index* arising from the study "accounts for 60% of the variance in explaining crisis preparedness" (p. 134).

**Gibbs Van Brunschot, E. E., & Sherley, A. J. (2005). Communicating threat: The Canadian state and terrorism.** *The Sociological Quarterly*, *46* **(4), 645–669**.

This article explores the Canadian response to the 9/11 crisis and asks how the government has been interpreting and communicating the terrorist threat to Canadians. A qualitative analysis of speeches and press releases on the website of the Prime Minister's Office was conducted, analysing content between September 2001 and October 2003 utilising a theoretical framework of *risk* and *trust* in an interpretivist approach. The researchers identified the categories of *threat, perpetrators, historical situation, Canada-United*

*States relationship*, among others, as main themes. Researchers also provide interesting interpretivist comparisons between Canadian and U.S. rhetorical approaches in terms of communicating terrorist threats.

Canadians have long held a fascination, whether rightly or wrongly, with their U.S. counterparts; comparisons between the two abound across almost every domain of study. Canadians are much more curious about such nuances, presumably in search of a clearer definition of their own distinctiveness. Such comparative studies satisfy these curiosities.

**Greenberg, M. (2005). The art of perpetuating a public health hazard.** *Journal of Occupational and Environmental Medicine, 47* **(2), 137–144**.

Greenberg outlines how the Canadian white asbestos industry relied heavily on PR to conceal the carcinogenic nature of the substance. Through an analysis of the deceptive PR techniques used to defend the substance, researchers present a cautionary analysis about the *masking strategies* that can be used in the public health sector.

**Johansen, P., & Ferguson, S. D. (2005). Canada, practice of public relations in. In R. L. Heath (Ed.),** *Encyclopedia of public relations* **(Vol. 2, pp. 112–116). Sage Publications**.

Relying primarily on Emms (1995), the authors provide a broad overview of PR development in Canada, citing PR activity since the 1600s by Samuel de Champlain.

**Kugler, M. (2005). What can be learned from case studies in public relations? An analysis of eight Canadian lobbying campaigns.** *Journal of Communication Management, 9* **(1), 73–88**.

Applying a typology of case studies on eight award-winning PR case studies and accreditation samples from the archives of the CPRS, Kugler suggests such a typology can be refined or developed as a tool to adjudicate *excellence* in PR practice.

This is an example of some of the research coming out of francophone Université Laval, Québec City, Québec. Education, scholarship and practice occurring in the PR francophone community needs to be comparatively researched and even translated for greater accessibility and knowledge dissemination.

**Lamertz, K., Heugens, P., & Calmet, L. (2005). The configuration of organizational images among firms in the Canadian beer brewing industry.** *Journal of Management Studies, 42* **(4), 817–843**.

Utilising the theoretical framework of *organisational image management*, researchers examined the websites of 36 breweries in Ontario and Québec to conceptualise and operationalise *identity formation* attributes. Researchers wished to identify how organisations position themselves to outward-facing publics to achieve a positive image. The researchers developed a complex typology of systems with maps and models. Empirical studies utilising typologies, statistical analysis and content analysis are needed to advance the discipline and firmly establish it in scholarship.

**Blazer, T. (2006) 'In case the raid is unsuccessful . . .' Selling Dieppe to Canadians.** *The Canadian Historical Review, 87* **(3), 409–430.**

Blazer examines the claim that the Canadian government engaged in a program of disinformation about the failed 1942 Dieppe attack as a means to manage public perceptions and prevent a public inquiry. Blazer engages in critique about the unseemliness of deceptive messages in the public sphere.

While the terms *misinformation* or *malinformation* or *disinformation* did not exist in 2006, this study becomes relevant today in an age where such terms have entered the lexicon. Additionally, PR scholars have many current contexts in which to study the dynamics and dangers of unethical messaging.

**Breton, G., & Côté, L. (2006). Profit and the legitimacy of the Canadian banking industry.** *Accounting, Auditing & Accountability Journal, 19* **(4), 512–539.**

Public opinion and perception of the banking industry was examined over a 50-month period in light of questionable practices that threatened *consumer trust* and *organisational legitimacy*. The researchers concluded that responses by the banking industry to a barrage of negative media coverage were largely ineffective, demonstrating ineffective communication efforts.

**Cooper, J. (2006).** *Crisis communications in Canada: A practical approach.* **Centennial College Press.**

This textbook, suitable for a crisis communications class, begins with a North American overview, highlighting such U.S. classics as the Johnson & Johnson Tylenol case. The author launches into Canadian and examples of RBC crisis of 2004 when customers became locked out of their accounts; cougars threatening Alberta residents; Saskatchewan Chemical's industrial spill; the Canadian flag controversy in Newfoundland and Labrador in 2004; the Canadian government and the avian flu; fire at Horizon Plastics in Ontario; the Mississauga train derailment; Natrel and the contaminated milk crisis; the banning of pit bulls in Ontario; and others. The textbook is very practical with many tools, tips and discussion prompts. Offering a host of Canadian examples, it is now in its second edition (Cooper, 2015).

**Flynn, T. (2006). A delicate equilibrium: Balancing theory, practice and outcomes.** *Journal of Public Relations Research, 18* (2), 191–201.

In this commentary, a Canadian PR scholar offers challenges on future directions of PR research. Rooted in pragmatism, Flynn proposes a move away from *two-way symmetrical* thinking "to reconceptualize public relations in a multi-dimensional perspective where dialogue, collaboration and negotiation with multiple stakeholders and stakeseekers occur simultaneously and that the new role of the public relations practitioner is to maintain an equilibrium that satisfies the mutual interest of all parties" (p. 193). Secondly, Flynn puts forward a view of *balance*, identifying nine initial factors from PR scholarship to consider in the creation of a *balanced zone* of PR practice that takes all factors into consideration as a form of excellent practice. Thirdly, Flynn challenges scholars to

> demonstrate the outcomes and relationships that public relations facilitates for organisations to enhance their reputation . . . to qualify and quantify the outcomes of our programs to demonstrate the effect that they have in helping the organisation to achieve its goals and objectives.
>
> (p. 197)

He warns against overemphasis on the study of enhanced reputation, however, as "reputation follows relationship, and relationships are a direct outcome of public relations/communications management" (p. 198).

Flynn's challenge propels PR scholarship forward by challenging scholars to think beyond the two-way approaches that have formed the theoretical foundations of both scholarship and practice, and which are already firmly entrenched. Flynn points out that the foundation of PR is contained within its moniker: *relations-ships*. This hearkens to groundbreaking sentiment by Ferguson (1984, 2018) and subsequent reminders by Hon and Grunig (1999) that PR scholarship should, at its most basic, study the nature and quality of the relationship between an organisation and its publics. Flynn echoes this call.

**Killeen, R. (2006). Public relations for pharmacists 101 staying 'on message'.** *Canadian Pharmacists Journal*, 7–8.

This commentary, by a member of the medical profession, argues against the need for formal PR campaigns for pharmacists since, according to Killeen, pharmacists engage in PR daily, forming the basis of reputation and image management. Killeen argues that since consumers shape public policy, the most important PR work by pharmacists arises out of the quality of daily pharmacist-consumer interactions, concluding that formal PR campaigns, therefore, are not necessary.

Canada's medical community has been shown to be somewhat averse to marketing efforts in medicine (see, for example, Trent, 1991). Killeen's opinions mirror and support this tendency.

The reason for this view may be rooted in the foundational structure of the healthcare system in Canada; it is government-funded and does not overtly rely on marketing to attract users. Questions for PR researchers are: What are the best theories and methods by which healthcare practitioners in Canada's system establish good will, build reputation, create a positive image and maintain trust? In such a system, what are the factors that threaten or destroy trust? And, if trust is diminished, how can it be rebuilt in such a system?

**Vervoort, P. (2006). "Towers of silence": The rise and fall of the grain elevator as a Canadian symbol.** *Social History*, *39* (77), 181–204.

The grain elevator has become one of the iconic symbols of Canadian life. Vervoort examines this symbolism and the shared meaning it has evoked by tracing its evolution, national recognition and international admiration.

Even though these grain elevators are disappearing from the landscape, they provide an example of symbolism that is ingrained in much of the Canadian psyche. They also remind us of the many other symbols associated with Canada (e.g., maple leaf) and how strategic communicators can use these for effective communication. Examination into Canadian symbols and strategic communication both domestically and abroad can develop Canadian distinctiveness and add to the Canadian PR narrative.

**Barratt, N. (2007).** *Chocolate milk is good for you: Video news releases, PR and knowledge production in Canadian television journalism* [Master's thesis, Concordia University]. **Library and Archives Canada.**

Barratt argues that video news releases produced by PR sources are problematic in that they are not vetted for journalistic standards, and sources can be obscure.

Newsrooms in Canada have continued to face challenges since the development of online journalism. Studies that examine a possible changing relationship between PR and journalism in Canada, and other implications of the evolving landscape, are warranted.

**Elliott, G., & Charlebois, S. (2007). How Mosaic-Esterhazy applied a crisis communication strategy when it suddenly had the world's attention.** *Public Relations Review*, *33* (3), 319–325.

This article systematically outlines and analyses effective crisis management in the case of 72 trapped miners in Esterhazy, Saskatchewan.

Most significantly, the authors found that Mosaic-Esterhazy quickly and effectively utilised the media to create an open two-way dialogue with the public. Other key success points identified in the crisis communication process included *preparedness, honesty, transparency, absence of blame-shifting* and *calmness*. The authors also identified the important role of teleconference calls that provided direct lines of communication to miners' families. Ironically, Mosaic had neither a dedicated spokesperson, nor a comprehensive crisis plan; yet, this crisis management has been recognised internationally as 'almost-faultless' and the benchmark for mine safety.

**Givel, M. (2007). A comparison of the impact of U.S. and Canadian cigarette pack warning label requirements on tobacco industry profitability and public health.** *Health Policy, 83* (2), 343–352.

Givel analyses Canadian and U.S. legislation regarding warnings on cigarette packaging to judge the effectiveness of encouraging smoking cessation. Givel argues that Canadian cigarette pack warning labels are more effective owing to the stronger warnings required by Canadian legislation.

**Jahansoozi, J. (2007). Organisation – public relationships: An exploration of the Sundre petroleum operators group.** *Public Relations Review, 33* (4), 398–406.

The researcher explores the nature of the OPR within Sundre Petroleum Operators Group through a qualitative study of industry and community members. Results indicated the primary factor for building and maintaining relationships was *trust*.

This is an example of what researchers such as Ferguson (1984, 2018) and Flynn (2006) have challenged PR scholars to strive for; that is, examination of the *relationship* aspect of *public relations*. Methods to measure the quality of professional relationships have been provided by scholars like Hon and Grunig (1999).

**LaVigne, M. (2007).** *Making ink and airtime: How to conduct proactive media relations in Canada.* **Hunter LaVigne Communications**.

LaVigne situates media relations within PR. He examines its relationship to marketing and discusses newsworthiness, challenges faced by journalists, media relations in French Canada, media uses and gratifications, tips on practice, social media, writing and case studies. He suggests that the practice of media relations efforts must format and present information in the manner dictated by the channel being used and in accordance with how the end user consumes media. The book is in its third edition as LaVigne (2020).

**Stanbridge, K. (2007). Framing children in the Newfoundland confedera-tion debate, 1948.** *The Canadian Journal of Sociology, 32* (2), 177–201.

Utilising the theoretical orientation of *framing*, Stanbridge explores the use and depictions of children during the pro- and anti-Confederate movement of 1948. Pro-Confederate messaging used the frame of children's health and well-being as being associated with advancing efforts toward Confederation of the prov-ince with the rest of Canada. Anti-Confederates challenged this depiction as an incorrect foundation upon which to make a political decision.

Framing studies are a staple in PR research. Stanbridge suggests that fram-ing can be restricted or constrained by cultural considerations. This opens possibilities for framing studies that consider the role of culture. Canada, of-ten called a cultural *mosaic* and steeped in the multicultural policies carved out by Prime Minister Pierre Elliott Trudeau in the 1970s, provides a rich context for such comparative studies.

**Flynn, T., Gregory, F., & Valin, J. (2008).** *CPRS public relations definition and values.*www.cprs.ca/aboutus/mission.aspx

A small group of Canadian practitioners and academics came together to carve out a Canadian definition of PR:

> Public relations is the strategic management of relationships between an organisation and its diverse publics, through the use of communication, to achieve mutual understanding, realise organisational goals and serve the public interest.
>
> (Flynn et al., 2008)

This definition carries the concepts of *diversity*, *mutuality* and *public inter-est*; it points toward a particular set of societal values. This, in itself, poses interesting research questions: What does this definition say about Canadian practice, practitioners or research? Why? Does it reflect current realities?

**Hudson, S., Hudson, D., & Peloza, J. (2008). Meet the parents: A parents' perspective on product placement in children's films.** *Journal of Business Ethics, 80* (2), 289–304.

This article analyses product placement and advertising in children's films from the parents' perspective, utilising a four-point typology. Parents judged the *explicit placement of ethically charged products* to be unethical (to vary-ing degrees) and were in favour of more regulation around the use of product placements that could affect children.

PR work can include the securing of product placements in television, movies or other media (Cision, 2022). Since the CBC is mandated to produce a selection of Canadian-specific content, this topic can be examined for the nature of any specific product placements, the intentions of the sponsors and any effects upon Canadian audiences.

**McKenzie-Brown, P., Rennie, J., & CPRS Calgary (Eds.). (2008).** *Barbecues, booms & blogs: 50 years of public relations in Calgary.* **Detselig Enterprises.**

Produced in honour of the 50th anniversary of the CPRS, this is a collection of articles reflecting on the history and development of the organisation including case studies. It also contains many memories and stories of practitioners. The title is reminiscent of a common practice among many PR practitioners in Calgary, Alberta, who, in the 1970s, gathered regularly to socialise and share their PR stories at backyard barbecues.

**Basen, I. (2009). Round table counter-spin: A response to Boyd Neil.** *Canadian Journal of Communication, 34* **(2), 311–313. Also, Neil, B. (2009). Round table Spin Cycles unspun.** *Canadian Journal of Communication, 34* **(2), 307–310.**

These entries are grouped together as an exchange between Neil and Basen based on Basen's six-part radio drama series *Spin Cycles: A Series about Spin, the Spinners and the Spun.* The program dishes up the field of PR to the general public, introducing listeners to the history of the field and the realities of its challenges. Basen openly states his view on the reasons for the stigma surrounding the field, providing a critical view. Neil defends. Neil challenges Basen for his critical views about PR practice and history, but Basen defends himself and reiterates his commitment to portraying balanced views of both PR and journalism. Neil acknowledges that the radio series would be good listening by students of PR.

**Cadence, B. (2009). Heeding the warning signs: Investigating crisis communications at Trent University in the aftermath of Virginia Tech.** *The McMaster Journal of Communication, 6* **(1), 13–32.**

Four leaders of Trent University in Ontario were interviewed to examine the effects of the university shooting at Virginia Tech in Blacksburg, Virginia, on the crisis management planning at their own university. The reported effects were a) heightened awareness; b) realisation of the need for a campus-wide broadcasting/communication system; c) development of a campus violence reporting policy; d) reinforcement of the need for timely and transparent communication; e) strengthened relationships with first-responders; and f) more finely tuned crisis communications plans, among others. This case study revealed that parallel crises can have substantial impacts on an organisation's crisis plans if crisis planners are willing to examine outside crises and adapt.

**Ferguson, H. (2009). The environmental scan in corporate citizenship.** *McMaster Journal of Communication, 6* **(1).**

Ferguson proposes a management tool, *The Environmental Scan in Corporate Citizenship*, for corporate planners to engage in thoughtful CSR. The tool is underpinned in theoretical concepts, and Ferguson makes the case that more structured approaches and scanning systems can guide managers in their CSR efforts.

**Fletcher, J. F., Bastedo, H., & Hove, J. (2009). Losing heart: Declining support and the political marketing of the Afghanistan mission.** *Canadian Journal of Political Science, 42* **(4), 911–937.**

Researchers examined public opinion surveys to account for an abrupt drop in support for Canadian military missions in Afghanistan. Through regression analysis, researchers determined the reasons for the loss of public support to be a) pre-existing public sentiment; b) the acquisition of political information; and c) the role of emotion. Support for the Afghanistan mission was fractured along lines of those with a *realist orientation* and those with a *peacekeeping outlook*. Researchers found that a) Canadians engage foreign policy issues at an emotional level; b) Canadians are receptive to information about international affairs provided to them by their government; and c) Canadians carefully consider what their country's role in foreign affairs should be.

**Flynn, T., & Sévigny, A. (2009). The paradox of public relations/communications management education in Canada: Taught but not studied.** *McMaster Journal of Communication, 6* **(1).**

Flynn and Sévigny outline the state of PR and communications scholarship and education within Canada. This article notes the comparative lack of empirical research about PR in Canada and a lack of research-led graduate programs with no clearly outlined collection of knowledge on the subject. Hence, they agree with Johansen's judgement (2001) that the field is only semi-professional. They argue for more studies that focus on empirical evidence and the further development of graduate-level work based on both theory and practice.

The *McMaster Journal of Communication*, developed by the researchers, represents a development in PR scholarship in Canada. Developed in 2004 out of the Faculty of Humanities at McMaster University in Hamilton, Ontario, it expanded with the development of a graduate program in 2009. A sister publication, *The Journal of Professional Communication*, was launched in 2011, also to support the graduate program and provide a quality venue for the publication of strategic communication research by students, academics or industry practitioners. These journals provide publication possibilities for high-quality submissions, thus encouraging the development of PR research in Canada, which has increased since the inception of these journals.

**Greenberg, J., & Elliott, C. (2009). A cold cut crisis: Listeriosis, Maple Leaf Foods, and the politics of apology.** *Canadian Journal of Communication, 34* (2), 189–204.

Greenberg and Elliot analyse the crisis response strategy of Maple Leaf Foods in the aftermath of a listeriosis crisis through the framework of *organisational legitimacy*. The strategy used was one of *high visibility* and *immediate full apology*, to positive effect.

This crisis represented one of the worst health and food contamination cases in Canadian history to that date and garnered much media attention. Maple Leaf Foods became Canada's 'textbook case' as an exemplar of excellent practice in the Canadian context (see Gorney, 2002). This case also demonstrated the power of public apology in an environment where legal advisors held prominent sway and tended to advise silence. Public apologies for misdeeds became fairly commonplace during this time, such as in the case of golfer Tiger Woods (Araton, 2010). As of this writing, Maple Leaf Foods continues to enjoy a positive reputation in Canadian society.

**Greenberg, J., & MacAulay, M. (2009). NPO 2.0? Exploring the web presence of environmental nonprofit organizations in Canada.** *Global Media Journal, 2* (1), 63–88.

The researchers examined digital communications (Facebook, Twitter, RSS feeds, blogs) of 43 environmental nonprofit organisations that were members of the group Climate Action Network-Canada, showing that *two-way dialogic* approaches of communication were not being extensively used and communication opportunities were being missed.

With the advent of new media (websites) in the 1990s and then social media around 2006, PR scholarship has been addressing these major communications developments, albeit slowly. This represents an early empirical study about social media use in Canada utilising content analysis.

**Killingsworth, C. (2009). Municipal government communications: The case of local government communications.** *McMaster Journal of Communication, 6* (1), 61–79.

The researcher explored the role and value of communication at the level of local government in Canada by studying the case of a large municipality in Western Canada. Utilising in-depth interviews of government officials and workers, the study suggested that a) the importance of the role and value of communication is often acknowledged, but not by all; b) many government offices do not have large communications staffs or capabilities; c) two-way communication is valued and practised in the form of surveys and social media tools, with one-way approaches present; d) representatives were interested in measurement and evaluation but often lacked the data needed; e) the communication function is not part of the dominant coalition; f) respondents believed their messaging was effective with the general public; and g) the municipality showed many of the hallmarks of *Excellence Theory*.

**Likely, F. (2009). A different country, a different public relations: Canadian PR in the North American context. In K. Sriramesh & D. Vercic (Eds.), *The global public relations handbook: Theory, research and practice* (pp. 674–775). Routledge.**

Likely's chapter proposes a timeline of PR development in Canada and adds to the comparative lack of research on the history of PR in the country. Likely suggests five periods of evolutionary development: 1604–1900, 1900–1940, 1940–1945, 1945–1970, and 1970 to time of publication. The author also assesses the political, economic and legal environments. Likely additionally uses a case study to illustrate the view that the Canadian tendency is for *evolutionary change* over *revolutionary violence*. Likely points to the *two-way symmetrical model* as a somewhat typical Canadian approach.

Likely's view echoes Guiniven (2002) and Johansen (2001) who also identify Canadian approaches as akin to *two-way symmetrical* models of communication. Some empirical research and further study is needed to tease out this Canadian distinctiveness, contributing to other narratives about PR practice in Canada.

**Morris, K. T. (2009). Crisis communications: Challenges faced by remote and rural communities in North Eastern Ontario. *The McMaster Journal of Communication*, 6 (1), 82–100.**

Morris interviewed staff of a healthcare organisation in Ontario to determine the most effective tools for crisis communication considering the challenges of remoteness, distance, low population density, technological challenges and weather. Morris confirmed the hypothesis that traditional forms of communications (telephones, media) were most utilised and effective for use in remote areas. The communication method of personal interaction was most preferred by workers and considered to be more effective than technology-based tools because technology was reportedly not always available.

**Potter, E. H., & Ebook Central – Academic Complete. (2009, 2008, 2014). *Branding Canada: Projecting Canada's soft power through public diplomacy*. McGill-Queen's University Press.**

Globalisation and communications have necessitated that countries become more aware of their own brands on the international stage. Potter examines

Canada's branding, diplomacy and use of soft power, somewhat chastising the nation for underperformance. Potter argues that Canada can be more proactive in the realm of public diplomacy, capitalising on its positive international image. Potter points to such national assets as intellectual leadership in peacekeeping, communication technology and mediation.

**Pullen, H. (2009). The relationship between public relations and marketing in the nonprofit Sector: The case of Hamilton Health Sciences and Hamilton Health Sciences Foundation. *The McMaster Journal of Communication, 6* (1), 103–119.**

Pullen examined the relationship between a PR department and a marketing department as a case study in a nonprofit setting. Results showed a positive synergy between the two departments to achieve organisational goals. There were differences of opinion about the definition of PR and the suggestion that the two departments should merge; there was also a suggestion for stronger boundaries between the two functions.

This study is indicative of ongoing discussions about distinctions between PR and marketing and their respective roles within organisations, which has been discussed since the inception of PR scholarship (Kotler & Mindak, 1978; Hutton, 1999; DeSanto & Mathis, 2014).

**Thurlow, A. (2009). "I just say I'm in advertising": A public relations identity crisis? *Canadian Journal of Communication, 34* (2), 245–263.**

Thurlow studied the *sensemaking* processes of PR professionals as they constructed their *professional identities*, particularly in light of stigma and negative views around the profession (e.g., 'spin doctors'). A series of six semi-structured interviews were conducted as the basis for the interpretivist discussion finding that a) the issue of ethics was of central concern to professional identity; b) females were not part of the dominant coalitions; and c) professional identity construction was a complex process.

**Villegas, N. (2009). Assessing reputation management, internal communications and perceptions in Oakville, Ontario. *The McMaster Journal of Communication, 6* (1), 131–143.**

Five executives of major Canadian companies were interviewed about their views on internal communications. Some findings were that a) executives associated *communication* in terms of external audiences rather than internal; b) internal communication tended to come from marketing officers or human resource officers versus communications officers; and c) person-to-person communication was diminishing in favour of electronic communication.

# References

Araton, H. (2010, February 19). Apologizing, woods sets no date for return to golf. *The New York Times.* www.nytimes.com/2010/02/20/sports/golf/20woods.html

Cancel, A., Cameron, G., Sallot, L., & Mitrook, M. (1997). It depends: A contingency theory of accommodation in public relations. *Journal of Public Relations Research, 9*(1), 31–63.

Carney, W. W., Babiuk, C., & LaVigne, M. H. (2019). *In the news: The practice of media relations in Canada* (3rd ed.). University of Alberta Press.

Cision. (2022, July 17). PR Newswire expands sponsored placement network of premium publishers to Europe and Canada. *PR Newswire Asia.* ProQuest.

Coatney, C. (2012). Public relations techniques for leaders in a crisis: Mackenzie King and John Curtin in the Canadian-Australian war alliance, 1941–1945 1. *Global Media Journal, 5*(2), 5–22.

Cooper, J. (2015). *Crisis communications in Canada: A practical approach* (2nd ed.). Centennial College Press.

DeSantos, B., & Mathis, C. B. (2014). How public relations and advertising continue to grow and live together. In H. Cheng (Ed.), *The handbook of international advertising research* (pp. 484–509). John Wiley & Sons, Ltd.

Emms, M. J. (1995). *The origins of public relations as an occupation in Canada* [Master's Thesis, Concordia University, Montreal].

Ferguson, M. A. (1984, August). *Building theory in public relations: Interorganizational relationships as a public relations paradigm* [Paper presentation]. AEJMC, Gainesville, FL.

Ferguson, M. A. (2018). Building theory in public relations: Interorganizational relationships as a public relations paradigm. *Journal of Public Relations Research, 30*, 164–178.

Gorney, C. (2002). The mystification of the Tylenol crisis. *The Public Relations Strategist, 8*(4), 21–25.

Grunig, J. E., & Hunt, T. (1984). *Managing public relations.* Holt, Rinehart and Winston.

Hon, L., & Grunig, J. E. (1999). *Guidelines for measuring relationships in public relations.* www.instituteforpr.com/pdf/1999_guide_measure_relationships.pdf

Hutton, J. G. (1999). The definition, dimensions, and domain of public relations. *Public Relations Review, 25*(2), 199–214.

Kotler, P., & Mindak, W. (1978). Marketing and public relations: Should they be partners or rivals? *Journal of Marketing, 42*(4), 13–20.

Kugler, M. (2010). *Des campagnes de communication réussies, Tome 2: 42 études de cas primés.* Presses de l'Université du Québec.

LaVigne, M. H. (2020). *Proactive media relations: A Canadian perspective.* Centennial College Press.

Shade, L. R. (2014). *Mediascapes: Mew patterns in Canadian communication* (4th ed.). Nelson.

Sommers, S. (2009). *Building media relationships: How to establish, maintain and develop long-term relationships with the media* (2nd ed.). Oxford University Press.

Trent, B. (1991). Psychiatrists confront an image problem. *Canadian Medical Association Journal, 144*(12), 1651–1655. www.ncbi.nlm.nih.gov/pmc/articles/PMC1335541/pdf/cmaj00241-0061.pdf

Wright, N. K. (1976). The challenge of public relations in Canada. *Public Relations Quarterly, 21*(3), 23–25.

# 5  2010s

- This decade saw a surge of scholarship mainly because of the work of graduate students. With the launch of the inaugural issue of the *Journal of Professional Communication* in 2011, funded by a grant from the Social Sciences and Humanities Research Council, PR and communications scholarship was accelerated. Five of the 12 articles and briefs in the inaugural edition were felt to be highly PR-oriented and in the Canadian context, and appear here. In 2014, a sister publication, *McMaster Journal of Communication*, dedicated an entire issue, *Engaging Publics*, to PR-oriented content in Canadian contexts. Following, in March 2018, the *Canadian Journal of Communication* dedicated an entire issue to communication and the energy industry.
- Important developments include explorations into social media. (See Basha, 2011; Brunsdon, 2011; Smitko, 2012.)
- There is also theoretical development during this decade in terms of decolonisation (Kenny, 2018), which is an important Canadian theme and distinctive. Government communication and crisis communication remain of high interest.
- The intersection of PR and religion begins to be explored. (See Mix-Ross, 2011; Selby, 2013; Shepard, 2014.)
- The *Report of the Generally Accepted Practices (VIII) Survey (Canadian)* was a key development in the documentation and study of practice in Canada (Thurlow et al., 2014).
- Carney and Lymer (2015) published an influential and comprehensive textbook.
- The decade saw greater interest in Canadian contexts, and possibilities for new narratives (e.g., decolonisation) are emerging. Due to the volume of works in this chapter, annotations are brief.

**Canadian Public Relations Society. (2010).** *60 years, 60 milestones: The Canadian Public Relations Society: A history of development and achievement.* **Canadian Public Relations Society**.

Prepared for its 60th anniversary, CPRS contributors document their history, milestones and challenges. This is a key document about the development of PR in the country.

DOI: 10.4324/9781003507475-8

**DuHamel, C. (2010).** *Disclosure and organisational transparency: A model for communication management* [Doctoral thesis, University of Stirling].

DuHamel's research proposes a model for communications management in disclosure situations. Key themes from interviews and focus groups of 22 senior communicators were tested to refine the model, which is based on *transparency*, *ethics* and *two-way symmetry*, balancing the needs of stakeholders and supporting *Excellence Theory*.

**Dumas, M. (2010).** *Les relations publiques, une profession en devenir.* **Presses de l'Université du Québec.**

This is an overview, in French, of the evolution of the discipline from a North American perspective with a focus on Canada in Chapter Five. Some examination and translation of materials across the French and English languages for knowledge sharing would make such works more accessible and pose some research questions.

**Kugler, M. (2010).** *Des campagnes de communication réussies. 42 études de cas primés, tome 2.* **Presses de l'Université du Québec.**

This is Volume 2 (also see Kugler, 2004) in a set; it systematically reviews 42 award-winning campaigns conducted from 2003–2007. Designed as a textbook, this provides francophone students of PR with a scientifically based method of PR case analysis.

**Petruk, J. (2010). Awareness campaigns do make a difference.** *Canadian Nurse, 106* **(5), 32–33.**

Petruk examines a media and digital campaign, *Expert Caring Makes a Difference*, conducted by an Alberta nursing association to promote the value and role of registered nurses. Positive public opinion increased from 89% to 97%. The author urges nurses to engage in storytelling as a way to continue the positive impact and effects of the campaign. Research into the various aspects of the medical system can be explored in the distinctive context of Canada's largely government-funded healthcare system.

**Basha, J. C. (2011).** *Social media, public relations and the Government of Canada: An analysis of internal organizational texts* [Masters thesis, Mount Saint Vincent University].

Basha examines the government's social media policy through the lens of *structuration theory* and determined that mechanistic government structures and communications practices were incongruent with rapidly advancing social media technologies, thus hindering government communications at the federal level.

**Berry, J., Cole, R. T., & Hembroff, L. (2011). US-Canada study of PR writing by entry level practitioners reveal significant supervisor dissatisfaction.** *Journal of Professional Communication, 1* (1), 57–77.

Members of the CPRS were interviewed regarding the skill level of entry level PR practitioners and results compared to a prior study of both U.S. and Canadian supervisors. Results showed overall dissatisfaction. Researchers propose a curriculum that includes strong writing requirements, calling for longitudinal research.

**Blazer, T. (2011).** *The information front: The Canadian Army and news management during the Second World War.* **UBC Press.**

Blazer notes a dearth of study at the intersection of PR and war news by the Canadian Army. The researcher reviews the army's publicity and war messaging during WWII, focusing on Normandy, Sicily and Dieppe as case studies for analysis.

**Brunsdon, D. (2011). The gendered engagement of Canada's national affairs and legislative elite, online.** *Journal of Professional Communication, 1* (1), 81–97.

This study examined the gendered nature of digital media usage (Facebook, Twitter, LinkedIn, blogs) among a purposive sample of legislators, national journalists and lawyers. Women and men were found to be equally engaged in online activity; however, men were found to have a larger online following and fan base. Brunsdon argues that this can be attributed to social gendered favouritism and structural gender bias.

**CPRS National Council on Education. (2011). Pathways to the profession: An outcomes based approach to excellence in Canadian public relations and communications management education.** *Journal of Professional Communication, 1* (1), 211–241.

This is a foundational document to PR education in Canada, providing a framework and acknowledging many entry points into the profession – *technical, career, management, leadership* or *scholarship.*

**Dawson, M. (2011). A "civilizing" industry: Leo Dolan, Canadian tourism promotion, and the celebration of mass culture.** *The American Review of Canadian Studies, 41* (4), 438–447.

Dawson examines the rhetoric of Leo Dolan, a key figure in the Canadian Government Travel Bureau, whose mission was to expand tourism into Canada. Unlike the cultural critics of his day, Dolan championed tourism and mass culture as contributory to society and democratic ideals. These views represented part of the modern shift taking hold in society and business. Dawson's examination gives readers a view into shifting societal attitudes during post-war Canada.

**Francis, D. (2011).** *Selling Canada: Three propaganda campaigns that shaped the nation.* **Stanton Atkins & Dosil**.

This book traces the work of Clifford Sifton with the Canadian Pacific Railroad, in response to the ongoing need for concentrated publicity and promotion to attract European immigrants. It documents some of the earliest modern PR activities in Canada focused on immigration.

**Greenberg, J., Knight, G., & Westersund, E. (2011). Spinning climate change: Corporate and NGO public relations strategies in Canada and the United States.** *International Communication Gazette, 73* **(1–2), 65–82**.

Researchers evaluate the role of PR in the climate change debate, urging NGOs to more fully avail themselves of this function to achieve organisational objectives.

**Hoggan, J. (2011). Honest to goodness: Three simple rules to repair public mistrust of polluters.** *Alternatives Journal, 37* **(3), 20–21**.

Hoggan blames deceptive PR tactics for diminishing public trust in business with regard to environmental sustainability. Hoggan urges business leaders to look beyond the PR function by proposing a three-step strategy.

**Laing, A. (2011). The H1N1 crisis: Roles played by government communicators, the public and the media.** *Journal of Professional Communication, 1* **(1), 123–149**.

Laing examines crisis communications in Ontario amidst the swine flu incident of 2009 through the lens of *second-level agenda setting*.

**Mix-Ross, A. A. (2011).** *Fire in his belly: A history of the Office of Social Concerns and Public Relations of the Pentecostal Assemblies of Canada as coordinated by Reverend Hudson T. Hilsden, 1976–1993* **[Doctoral dissertation, Tyndale Seminary]**.

The researcher examines the internally controversial decision by a Canadian religious body to shift away from *advocacy* (lobbying, public education, media relations) and toward *general social concerns*. Studies at the intersection of PR and religion have not been widely explored, and this study opens such a door.

**Nanos, N. (2011). Polling in the 2011 Canadian federal election.** *Journal of Professional Communication, 1* **(1), 27–30.**

Nik Nanos, of Nanos Research, writes this commentary about the role of opinion research in federal elections, noting that polls can help politicians with issue selection and issue framing as well as help to contextualise media analyses. Nanos acknowledges the increasing role of social media in public opinion formation.

**Pullen, H. (2011). Eastern Health: A case study on the need for healthcare communications.** *Journal of Professional Communication, 1* **(1).**

Through an analysis of the events, media coverage and interview with a senior executive, Pullen writes a very detailed case study of reputation management efforts (focused on one-on-one communication) by Eastern Health Region after it was discovered that lab results 1997–2005 were not guaranteed to have been accurate. Such specific and detailed case studies can be used in a classroom environment. It also includes a timeline of events and responses.

**Seijts, G. H., & Roberts, M. (2011). The impact of employee perceptions on change in a municipal government.** *Leadership & Organization Development Journal, 32* **(2), 190–213.**

This article analyses *organisational change management* from the perspective of employees at a municipal government in Ontario. Successful change was dependent upon a) perceived sense of competence; b) opportunities to participate in decision-making; and c) respect in the workplace, among others. In an age of ongoing change, research into PR as change management, both in the nonprofit and for-profit sectors, is valuable.

**Sévigny, A. (2011). A reflection on the evolution of the field of professional communication.** *Journal of Professional Communication, 1* **(1), 1–12.**

This editorial in the inaugural issue of the journal outlines the foundational purpose of the journal noting concerns about the field and the increasing role of social media. The author notes three new bachelor of PR programs at Conestoga College, Humber College and University of Ottawa, and three existing graduate programs at McMaster University, Royal Roads and Mount Saint Vincent University. The editorial acknowledges the need for appropriate academic venues for publication of PR and communications research. This article provides a good overview of the academic situation in Canada and the role of the journal, which has played a key role in the acceleration of PR research. Research into the history and development of PR education in Canada, as well as comparative studies, and studies against evolving best practices in PR education are needed.

**Wright, D. K. (2011), History and development of public relations education in North America.** *Journal of Communication and Management*, *15* (3), 236–255.

This paper explores the development of PR education over time across the United States and Canada. Wright offers a unique perspective with background and experience in both countries.

**Anger, M. (2012). Evaluation and excellence in public relations: A case study.** *Journal of Professional Communication*, *2* (2), 35–61.

This is a case study of the restructuring of a New Brunswick health authority. The analysis revealed strengths in the *RACE model* to detect planning errors in the research phase of communications, demonstrating the usefulness of the model for case analysis.

**Basen, I. (Producer). (2012, June 26–July 31).** *Spin Cycles [Six-part Radio Series]*. **Canadian Broadcasting Corporation.**

*Spin Cycles* is a six-part series that takes a caustic view of PR, exploring the relationship between the press, PR and corporations. Basen also traces some of the history of PR and helps listeners understand the role and complexities of PR in society. Basen brings a basic understanding about PR to the general public and somewhat elevates it (amidst his criticisms). Therefore, this show provides a relatively balanced view of PR.

**Bregend-Heald, D. (2012). Vacationland: Film, tourism, and selling Canada, 1934–1948.** *Canadian Journal of Film Studies*, *21* (2), 27–48.

This study follows the history of the federal government's use of film to promote the country and encourage tourism. Themes included a) showcasing the hospitality and friendliness of Canadians; and b) featuring the natural environment. Symbolism and imagery (e.g., landscapes, Mounties, the maple leaf, grain elevators) factor heavily into the history of modern PR in Canada as part of key messaging. Studies that explore such themes would illuminate the Canadian story.

**Coatney, C. (2012). Public relations techniques for leaders in a crisis: Mackenzie King and John Curtin in the Canadian-Australian war alliance, 1941–1945 1.** *Global Media Journal*, *5* (2), 5–22.

This paper analyses the media techniques and strategies used by Australia's John Curtin and Canada's Mackenzie King during the war alliance of Canada and Australia in 1941–1945 to gain widespread public support for war, from the lens of *public sphere* and *power*. The researcher identifies key approaches (e.g., inclusive language, appeals to democracy and bilateralism, clear and accessible words and positively managed stage performance on news movie reels) that likely contributed to success. The author notes the pair's background in news management and journalism as likely positive contributing factors.

**Harvey, J., & Young, R. (Eds.). (2012).** *Image building in Canadian municipalities.* **McGill-Queen's University Press.**

Chapter contributors examine the interaction between government, business and stakeholders in the development of municipal images to achieve policy objectives.

**Kelly, S. (2012). PR lessons from the Ocean Ranger tragedy.** *Journal of Professional Communication, 2* **(1), 13–18.**

This is a narrative about the author's experiences with the sinking of the *Ocean Ranger* in 1982, which was one of Canada's worst maritime tragedies, which resulted in 84 deaths. Kelly emphasises the importance of compassion in PR work and argues that teaching students about the *CPRS Declaration of Principles* and *Codes and Ethics* is just one step in the process of creating empathetic practitioners. The creation of oral histories in the face of crisis can be powerful tools of education for developing practitioners and presents a research opportunity.

**Koop, R. (2012). Party constituency associations and the service, policy and symbolic responsiveness of Canadian members of parliament.** *Canadian Journal of Political Science, 45* **(2), 359–378.**

Through interviews of 46 political actors, Koop determined that *constituency associations* greatly enhance the work, communication, reputation and image of Canadian Members of Parliament.

**Smitko, K. (2012). Donor engagement through Twitter.** *Public Relations Review, 38* **(4), 633–635.**

Smitko explores how Twitter can be used for donor engagement. Tweets were analysed using discourse analysis, and a rhetorical framework of *logos, pathos, ethos, eucharistia (thanking)* and *repetition.* Smitko identifies *Social Networking Theory* and *Social Judgement Theory* as two underlying forces for success, acknowledging the significant potential of the use of Twitter for donor engagement.

**Trew, S. (2012).** *The CETA deception: How the Harper government's public relations campaign misrepresents the Canada-European Union Comprehensive Economic and Trade Agreement.* **Policy Commons, Canadian Electronic Library. CID: 20.500.12592/c8m16z**

This report criticises the 2012 Harper government and its free trade policy, judging the accompanying website to be more of a propaganda campaign to bolster the image of the trade agreement. Trew points to a lack of transparency and absence of two-way symmetric communications in the development of the policy and calls for different approaches by governments engaging in policy development.

**Yates, S., & Caron, M. A. (2012). La communication comme vecteur de l'acceptabilité sociale des grandes projets.** *Journal of Professional Communication, 2* **(2), 93–106**.

The researchers propose a theoretical framework by which to understand the co-creation of meaning towards public acceptance of major public works projects, utilising Québec-based examples. As next steps, the authors propose that the framework be operationalised as a measurement of *social legitimacy.*

**Bégin, D., & Charbonneau, K. (2013). Re-thinking the R.A.C.E. model for a social media world.** *Journal of Professional Communication, 2* **(2), 109–132.**

Utilising the case study of the social media activity of an Edmonton police officer, this practical paper illustrates how the *RACE model* is a linear model not well-suited to the transient and ever-changing social media context. Some practical steps and tools for the development of social media strategy are provided.

**Berry, J. (2013). Canadian public relations students' interest in government communication: An exploratory study.** *Management Research Review, 36* **(5), 528–544**.

Berry surveys 39 students and recent graduates from the PR program at Mount Royal University to reveal students' low interest in government communications work. The author suggests that government communications departments should better market themselves to communications students to secure quality future personnel.

**Braun, S. L., & Thomas, S. (2013). Student perceptions of the use of learning logs to teach public relations writing.** *Procedia – Social and Behavioral Sciences, 93,* **1456–1460**.

Researchers tested a pedagogical tool on 29 PR students, created to help improve writing skills. Students reported overall value in using the tool and felt it contributed to greater cognitive awareness and better writing.

Courchesne, D. (2013). Trade unions should R.A.C.E. to survive in the current communications culture. *Journal of Professional Communication*, *2* (1), 7–12.

This is a short case study examining labour relations communication in the case of a 2011 strike at McMaster University. The author argues that the *RACE model* can be an effective part of strategic communication in the context of labour unions.

Flynn, T., & Sévigny, A. (2013). A fool's errand: Separating critical and professional communication studies. In J. Greenberg & C. Elliott (Eds.), *Communication in question: Competing perspectives on controversial issues in communication studies* (pp. 49–56). Nelson.

Flynn and Sévigny argue that communication studies in Canada have a heavy focus on teaching *critical theory* and often neglect *administrative communication theory* and praxis, noting that both, in equal measure, are important to professional communications education.

Greenburg, J. (2013). Risk communication and the disclosure dilemma: The case of Ottawa's endoscopy infection 'scare'. *Journal of Professional Communication*, *2* (1), 53–75.

While standard risk communication studies normally recommend early and full disclosure for public health crisis management, Ottawa's public health authority only released a partial disclosure in this health incident. Greenburg defends this approach on the basis of a) lack of organisational resources; and b) low risk/possibility of adverse events.

Johansen, P., & Ferguson, S. D. (2013). Canada, practice of public relations in. In R. L. Heath (Ed.), *Encyclopedia of public relations* (2nd ed., Vol. 2, pp. 94–97). Sage.

Relying heavily on Emms (1995), the authors summarise and provide an overview of the development of PR in Canada.

Likely, F. (2013). Managing strategically: Canadian federal government communication branches evaluated against five of the 'Generic Principles of Public Relations'. *Journal of Professional Communication*, *3* (1).

Likely tested some principles of *Excellence Theory* on government communications departments through analysis of past benchmark studies of 16 branches of government across three time periods. Likely concluded that five of the principles of *Excellence Theory* could be found to determine government communications was, therefore, strategic.

**Males, A. M. (2013). What factors are important in formulating a community hospital's reputation?** *Journal of Professional Communication, 3* **(1), 125–155.**

Males analyses community hospitals and their reputations through the variables of a) vision and leadership; b) financial performance; and c) social responsibility. The results suggested that a new model for analysing reputation for medical settings was needed. The author concludes that corporate reputation models are not always applicable to hospital environments and further research is warranted to determine the relationship between personal experience, familial doctors and hospital reputation. The examination of PR in Canadian hospitals, as government-funded institutions, presents a line of research of interest to any country contexts based on similar systems.

**McLean-Cobban, W. (2013). Proof positive: Thought leadership in Canadian professional service firms.** *Journal of Professional Communication,* *3* **(1), 67–96.**

This study considers attitudes and activities by 70 Canadian professional service firms about thought leadership and reputation. Quantitative and qualitative methods were used to determine that professional firms a) were very concerned with thought leadership; b) attempted to measure it; and c) looked mainly to blogs and conference presentations as effective methods to convey thought leadership.

**Morris, K. (2013). Can non-profit organisations be good social citizens? Developing best practices for social responsibility in the Ontario health-care sector.** *Journal of Professional Communication, 3* **(1), 159–180.**

In this practical paper, Morris proposes a model of CSR for the nonprofit healthcare sector. Interviews of 15 senior executives in the health sector in Ontario revealed that CSR was a) beneficial to the organisation and its employees; b) challenging but necessary; and c) required excellent communication for success. Specific examples and a ten-step model is provided.

**Rath, T. (2013).** *Public relations & communication management: In search of a pedagogical model for the MBA curriculum in Canada* **[Masters thesis, Mount Saint Vincent University].**

Through in-depth interviews with business leaders, the author concludes that a public relations/communication management component is an important and necessary feature in a graduate level business program.

**Selby, J. A. (2013). Promoting the everyday: Pro-sharia advocacy and public relations in Ontario, Canada's "Sharia debate".** *Religions, 4* **(3), 423–442.**

Selby lays additional groundwork for the study of PR and religious organisations, noting in this case study that Canadian Muslims are becoming more aware of the need for PR and political lobbying.

**Vayid, I. (2013).** *Central bank communications before, during and after the crisis: From open-market operations to open-mouth policy.* **Bank of Canada Working Paper, No. 2013–41. Bank of Canada, Ottawa.**

Vayid traces the evolution of bank communications since the 1990s as it moved toward greater clarity and transparency and deal with threats.

**Béland, D. (2014). Developing sustainable urban transportation: Lesson drawing and the framing of Montreal's bike sharing policy.** *International Journal of Sociology and Social Policy, 34* **(7/8).**

The researcher uses government documents, interviews and media coverage in the case of Montreal's bike-sharing initiative to explore the process of *drawing lessons from other jurisdictions* and *framing* them palatably for acceptance in another jurisdiction, noting the importance of nationalistic and local key messaging (e.g., 'made in Québec'). This study suggests a possible entry point into some further research and discussion about PR in a specific region in Canada, and points to the diverse nature of PR processes in the country.

**Bélanger, C. H., Bali, S., & Longden, B. (2014). How Canadian universities use social media to brand themselves.** *Tertiary Education and Management, 20* **(1), 14–29.**

Researchers explore Canadian universities' use of Twitter and Facebook to connect with students. Twitter was used more to engage in two-way dialogue with students, while Facebook was utilised more for one-way communication such as posting university news and events.

**Bernard, C. (2014). On the road to success: Examining how youth shelters define and value relationships through the practice of two-way symmetrical communication as a method to increase the success-rate of youth recovery programs. A case study of Youth Without Shelter.** *McMaster Journal of Communication, Special Issue, Engaging Publics, 11,* **59–73.**

This research article is featured in the *Engaging Publics* special edition of the journal. The case study supports the use of the *two-way symmetrical model* of communication to achieve organisational mission.

**Bernardino, P. (2014). Adopting versus adapting a PR plan: Investigating why and how public relations plans must be adapted to specific publics. *McMaster Journal of Communication, Special Issue, Engaging Publics, 11,* 37–46.**

Bernardino makes the case that PR plans targeted at Québec needed to be customised to account for unique culture, media outlets and language. Additionally, it was noted that Québec-based audiences a) preferred to see localised data included with national statistics; and b) have their own regional celebrities and recognised spokespeople they prefer to see showcased.

   This research illustrates that Canada is a diverse country, and there is a need for greater exploration of PR processes in various regions across various cultures toward the development of unique narratives. See also Béland (2014) earlier, for example.

**Berry, J. (2014). Y in the workplace: Comparative analysis of values, skills and perceptions of government communication amongst university students and government staff. *Foresight: The Journal of Future Studies, Strategic Thinking and Policy, 16* (5), 432–447.**

Student characteristics were studied as potential government communications workers. While students indicated they valued the role of government in their lives, they were not inclined toward a future working in government communications. Ongoing examination into who will fill communications positions within such governments is warranted and possibly predict the nature and trajectory of government communications practices in the future.

**Flynn, T. (2014). Do they have what it takes? A review of the literature on knowledge, competencies, and skills necessary for twenty-first-century public relations practitioners in Canada. *Canadian Journal of Communication, 39* (3), 361–384.**

Flynn engages in literature review to identify themes and core competencies for success in twenty-first-century PR practice. Written, oral and non-verbal communication skills are foundational, including professional writing ability across many channels and platforms. Other important skills include a) the ability to manage large amounts of information through information and communication technologies; b) the ability to engage in social listening; c) having well-developed ethical frameworks; d) strategic planning and measurement; e) cultural awareness; and f) collaboration skills.

**Kennedy, J. (2014). Relocation as a catalyst for change: How leadership empowered employees and achieved organisational change at Sanofi Canada. *Journal of Professional Communication, 4* (1), 71–97.**

This outlines a successful change management effort at Sanofi Canada, a global pharmaceutical company, as it went through re-location. Examination of PR as change management, utilising PR theory and principles, opens some lines of research.

**Koerber, D. (2014). Crisis communication response and political communities: The unusual case of Toronto mayor Rob Ford.** *Canadian Journal of Communication, 39* **(3), 311–331.**

Koerber challenges traditional crisis communication guidelines of *apologia* utilising the case of Toronto Mayor Rob Ford who was captured on video using illegal drugs. Koerber suggests that, in the political context, *denial* is necessary if supporters expect it. Koerber suggests that communication in the political context may need to be viewed differently than other crises.

**Kozolanka, K. (Ed.). (2014).** *Publicity and the Canadian state: Critical communications perspectives.* **University of Toronto Press**.

This volume of essays acknowledges the State's dependence on publicity and communication to retain legitimacy. Authors issue challenges and critiques of the relationship between PR and politics.

**Manley, D. (2014).** *The anxious profession: A study of competencies, qualifications and education in Canadian public relations* **[Masters thesis, Royal Roads University]**.

Manley's thesis explores the state of PR with regards to its security as a profession. Manley calls it an "anxious profession" because of underdevelopment of educational programs and a perception of limited value in professional accreditation.

**Manning, K. (2014).** *Pathways to a program: An examination of public relations education programs in Canada* **[Master's thesis, Mount Saint Vincent University]**.

Manning analysed the websites of 30 PR programs in Canada to determine which of the five pathways into the profession, as determined by CPRS (2011), were reflected in the programs. Most programs mirrored the first two pathways – *technical* and *career* – with little to no representation of the other three pathways – *management, leadership* or *scholarship*. Manning suggests a re-examination of the pathways document to be more reflective. More research into PR and strategic communications programs in Canada, both historical and present-day.

**Morgan, J. (2014). Destination ambassadors: Examining how hospitality companies value brand ambassadorship from front-line employees. A case study of Four Seasons Hotels and Resorts.** *The McMaster Journal of Communication, Special Issue, Engaging Publics, 11,* **75–108**.

Morgan uses the case study of the well-known luxury brand Four Seasons Hotels and Resorts to illustrate the impact of *hotel employee interactions with guests* to achieve *positive brand image*, portraying employees as important brand ambassadors for organisations.

**Shepard, J. R. (2014). An examination of how World Vision Canada communicates with publics of various ideological backgrounds and moves them to donate.** *The McMaster Journal of Communication, Special Issue, Engaging Publics, 11,* **3–34**.

Drawing upon *contingency theory*, *co-creation theory* and *community-building theory*, Shepard explores the case study of World Vision Canada, a Christian-based relief agency, to understand how the nonprofit organisation communicates with a broad range of publics. More exploration at the intersection of PR and faith-based institutions is needed.

**Braun, S. (2014). Can we all agree? Building the case for symbolic interactionism as the theoretical roots of public relations.** *Journal of Professional Communication, 4* **(1), 49–70**.

In a contested space, a Canadian academic sets out the case for symbolic interactionism as the theoretical origins of the field.

**Szustaczek, C. (2014). Turning belief into action: An exploratory case study applying the building belief model to an anonymous college in Ontario.** *Journal of Professional Communication, 4* **(1), 121–156**.

The researcher tests the readiness of an Ontario college to adopt a new corporate communications model. Gaps in readiness included lack of a strong, cohesive organisational culture and low levels of word-of-mouth sharing with external audiences, among others. Recommendations included that college leaders a) more clearly define the organisational character; b) develop stronger employee feedback and engagement; c) engage early influencers; and d) embrace storytelling.

**Thurlow, A., Kushniryk, A., Yue, A., & Blotnicky, K. (2014).** *Gap (VIII) Canada report 2014: Report of the generally accepted practices (VIII) survey (Canadian).*

This is the first extensive benchmark study documenting the state of PR practice in Canada, based on 122 responses. It was built upon a framework developed by researchers at University of Southern California and included Canada, Brazil, Australia, South Africa, New Zealand and the United States. Called the *GAP Study*, it was designed to be a biennial study conducted to document practice and pinpoint trends in participating countries around the world. The Canadian portion was executed as a joint venture between Mount Saint Vincent University, CPRS, *Canadian + Public Relations Foundation* and Global Alliance. This is an important key benchmark study about PR in Canada and a first of its kind.

**Unruh, H., & Savage, P. (2014). From MBA to MCM: A pedagogical examination of blended residency-online teaching and learning in a graduate professional communications program. *Journal of Professional Communication, 4* (1), 99–119.**

This study is a self-examination of the hybrid teaching model at McMaster University's Master of Communication program developed in partnership with Syracuse University. The study revealed the graduate program aligned very much with the literature best practices. Hybrid models were felt to be particularly appealing to mature professionals as long as there was a good balance between online learning and interpersonal engagement.

The issue of the effectiveness of online learning was accentuated during the COVID-19 period. Since that time, online learning has gained greater acceptance and has been integrated more into traditional classrooms (e.g., bringing in guest speakers digitally). As technologies continue to develop, the pedagogical role and value of various tools in the PR classroom needs to be continually examined.

**Weinstein, D. (2014). White Cashmere Collection 2013. *Journal of Professional Communication, 4* (1), 187–196.**

This is a case study of PR efforts around the re-branding of *Cottonelle* to *Cashmere Bathroom Tissue*. Success was experienced through integrated marketing and a CSR campaign involving Canadian designers and a fashion show.

**Wooding, C. (2014). The give and take of donor relations: Investigating the role communicators play in successful donor giving relationships. *McMaster Journal of Communication, Special Issue, Engaging Publics, 11*, 121–133.**

This paper explores the donor relations strategies of five successful nonprofit organisations in the Canadian agricultural sector. Specific mission, personal contact, regular communication and meaningful joint public outreach opportunities were highlighted as some suggested best practices.

Agriculture factors as a major part of the Canadian geography and experience. The intersection of PR and agriculture (with the exception of historical campaigns to attract immigrants) has not been widely explored.

**Yunusov, E. (2014). Effective watchdogs bark: The role of communications at the Office of the Ombudsman of Ontario.** *Journal of Professional Communication, 4* **(1), 21–27.**

Yunusov contributes to the growing literature around government communications by analysing communications within the Ombudsman Office in Ontario. Investigation into the role of Ombudsmen as mediators, through a PR lens, is warranted, particularly since the role, by its very nature, is a public relations one that involves the settling of disagreements through mediation or recommendation.

**Cardin, M., & McMullan, K. (2015).** *Canadian PR for the real world.* **Pearson.**

An educator and an industry expert team up to provide a practical textbook with Canadian examples, suitable for undergraduate classes as an introduction to PR.

**Carney, W. W., & Lymer, L. A. (2015).** *Fundamentals of public relations and marketing communications in Canada.* **The University of Alberta Press.**

This collective volume includes 16 chapters by 19 experts in their respective fields writing on strategic communication topics for students and practitioners. Topics include history, law, ethics, writing and crisis communication, among others. Carney's work has been recognized by CPRS, and this is a seminal textbook for Canadian students of strategic communication.

**Charest, F., & Bouffard, J. (2015). The characteristics of the e-influence of community managers: Issues for the e-reputation of organisations.** *Public Relations Review, 41* **(2), 302.**

Researchers surveyed 20 social media managers on LinkedIn in Québec to identify the perceived characteristics of successful e-influence that contribute to organisational reputation. Top-ranking characteristics were *personality, substantive content, omnipresence, community* and *credibility*. The *number of subscribers* ranked low.

**Golly, T., & Hnytka, P. (2015). Breaking barriers WITH building blocks: The story of the City of Edmonton's award-winning bicycle education videos.** *ITE Journal, 85* **(6), 19–23.**

This is a first-hand account by an engineer and a social marketer outlining the communication process by a municipality to educate the population on their new cycling infrastructure.

**McGrane, D., & Berdahl, L. (2015). Social unionism public relations and support for unions: A case study of public opinion in Saskatchewan, Canada. *Global Labour Journal, 6* (1), 62–78.**

A survey of Saskatchewan residents revealed that they were not opposed to unions if it was apparent that the union contributed to the public good. The author noted that *social unionism* is the dominant type of union in Canada. "The connection between public relations and Canadian social unionism has not been explored" (p. 65) even though "public relations and framing are increasingly important parts of union activity" (p. 66). The concept of *social unions* as public relations opens possibilities for Canadian PR distinctions.

**Thurlow, A. (2015). A critical historiography of public relations in Canada: Rethinking an ahistorical symmetry. In *The Routledge companion to management and organizational history* (pp. 302–315). Routledge.**

Thurlow critically examines *Excellence Theory* and its predominance within PR literature and calls for other narratives to document Canada's PR development, particularly in the areas of *ethics, professionalisation, Americanisation* and the *Canadian differentiation.*

This view forms some of the motivation and impetus behind this annotated bibliography.

**Braun, S. L. (2016). Social media use for public relations and reputation management in the university setting. In G. Okushova (Ed.), *Proceedings of the third international trans-disciplinary scientific and practical web conference, Connect Universum* (pp. 50–58). Publishing House of Tomsk State University.**

This is a case study of a Canadian university's experience with the adoption of social media for PR and reputation management, primarily among its students.

**Thurlow, A., & Yue, A. R. (2015). A brief history of PR in Canada. In W. W. Carney & L. A. Lymer (Eds.), *Fundamentals of public relations and marketing communications in Canada* (pp. 21–38). University of Alberta Press.**

The researchers provide a broad overview of the development of modern PR in Canada, drawing largely from Emms (1995) and integrating updated sources. More research into PR history in Canada is needed such as early agency activity, the impact of geography on PR development, biographies of leaders, statistics of agency and business development, corporate histories and Indigenous-Settler relations, among others.

**Killingsworth, C., & Flynn, T. (2016). Assessing the CPRS pathways to the profession competency framework: Perspectives on corporate communication leadership competencies and credentials.** *Corporate Communications, 21* (2), 177–194.

The researchers analyse *competency* and *leadership* within Canadian senior management through focus groups of 25 senior managers in four Canadian cities. The research found that the competency and credentials required for this profession, as outlined in *Pathways to the Profession*, were valid and valued within the existing corporate reality.

However, by comparison, Manley (2016) had more nuanced results with respect to the issue of perceived value of credentials. Further examination is needed.

**Lamberto, R. (2016). Police use of social media during a crisis.** *Journal of Professional Communication, 5* (1), 66–74.

Lamberto's study showed heavy reliance by police to communicate with the public using social media during a crisis. However, one major challenge was the need for additional staff to support.

**Manley, D. (2016). Crisis, what crisis? An overview of professional and academic credentials in Canadian public relations.** *Journal of Professional Communication, 5* (1), 135–153.

Interviews, surveys and content analysis of job postings were used to determine attitudes toward accreditation – either the Accredited Public Relations (ABC) designation or the Accredited Business Communicator (ABC) designation. This research, based on 22 interviews, 231 surveys and 600 job postings, found that practitioners preferred to obtain traditional graduate degrees over industry accreditations. The study further indicated employers valued formal education and work experience as the most important qualifications.

This study, when compared with Killingsworth and Flynn (2016), appears contradictory in terms of attitudes towards accreditation; however, this study has a much larger sample size. Research into evolving attitudes about accreditation would be beneficial.

**Parsons, P. (2016).** *Ethics in public relations: A guide to best practice* **(3rd ed.). Kogan Press.**

Written by a PR scholar based in Canada, this textbook offers a resource for the study of ethics in PR.

**Raso, K., & Neubauer, R. J. (2016). Managing dissent: Energy pipelines and "new right" politics in Canada.** *Canadian Journal of Communication,* *41* **(1), 115–133.**

The researchers examined news media discourse around the proposed Northern Gateway bitumen pipeline based on 853 samples, through the vantage points of *social network analysis* and *framing analysis*. In spite of many pro-pipeline media frames, the researchers predicted (correctly) that the pipeline would not be built. Their conclusion was based on reasons related to government policies, unresolved First Nations concerns and strong undercurrents of opposition, suggesting that dominant media frames do not necessarily predict outcomes.

**Stokes, J. (2016).** *The complete all-Canadian content-writing handbook.* **United States Blurb Incorporated.**

Through combining marketing and journalism skills, this is a manual written for PR, marketing and media practitioners, and includes writing tips and instructions.

**Thomlinson, J. (2016). Public relations as the new lobbyist rolodex.** *Journal of Professional Communication,* *5* **(1), 135–180.**

The author makes the case that *lobbying* is akin to *public relations* in line with *government relations*. Data was collected by interviews with 15 federally registered lobbyists and five senior communications managers, as well as a survey of 35 government relations workers. The literature review includes a brief history of lobbying in Canada and the United States. The author notes that social media is underutilised in lobbying in Canada.

**Antoine, D. (2017). Pushing the academy: The need for decolonizing research.** *Canadian Journal of Communication,* *42* **(1), 113–119.**

In this research brief, the writer encourages ongoing exploration of Indigenisation of the academy. A commitment toward decolonisation is a Canadian uniqueness that needs to be further explored in PR scholarship. Kenny (2018), however, opens the door by providing a suggested model.

**Batac, M. A. (2017). Teaching for social justice: Bringing activism into professional communication education.** *Canadian Journal of Communication,* *42* **(1), 139–142.**

The author laments personal experiences of pressures by communications students to receive their education from a strictly practical, corporatist perspective without significant desire for deeper exploration of matters related to PR for social justice issues and community needs.

The role of community service learning (which includes having students engage with community partners and nonprofit organisations to produce PR deliverables and outcomes) in PR education has yet to be formally researched. What are student experiences with this? What are partner organisations' experiences? What are challenges to implementation of such activities in PR education, and how can those challenges be addressed? How does community service learning contribute, specifically, to the readiness of the entry-level PR practitioner?

**Hawthorn, T. (2017).** *The year Canadians lost their minds and found their country: The Centennial of 1967.* **Douglas & McIntyre**.

Expo '67 was a defining moment in Canadian history and put the country on the world stage. Many of the communication and PR efforts behind this watershed event are discussed. These efforts are deserving of study as they can likely inform the national character and contribute to the developing narrative about the development of PR in Canada.

**Koerber, D. (2017).** *Crisis communication in Canada.* **University of Toronto Press, Higher Education Division**.

This textbook provides a foundational understanding of crisis communication theory within the Canadian context. This is a scholarly work filled with theory, references and Canadian examples.

**Marland, A. (2017). Above and below the line: Strategic communications and media management in Canadian governments.** *Canadian Public Administration, 60* **(3), 417–437**.

Marland explores the planning and strategising steps by the government in the preparation of media relations materials. Marland identifies *above the line* documents (media publications) and *below the line* documents (media calendars, plans, strategy). Findings also suggest there is less strategising associated with *urgent public safety and crisis communications* than with *routine communications.*

**Marland, A. (2017). Strategic management of media relations: Communications centralization and spin in the Government of Canada.** *Canadian Public Policy, 43* **(1), 36–49. https://doi.org/10.3138/cpp.2016-037**.

Marland asks if media communications will continue to be as controlled by the incoming federal government of Justin Trudeau as compared to that of the former Stephen Harper government. Data were collected from 17 confidential in-depth interviews of Harper government insiders. Marland concludes that some aspects of Harper's media control strategies and tools were less apparent in the Trudeau government. The researcher notes a paucity of study about government communication from an insider perspective.

**Oldfield, N. D., & Kushniryk, A. (2017). Building and protecting organizational trust with external publics: Canadian senior executives' perspectives.** *Canadian Journal of Communication, 42* **(5), 767–784.**

Researchers from Mount Vincent University interviewed 10 senior executives to determine how Canadian organisations generate trust. They identified eight factors: a) listening; b) clear, simple communication; c) reliability; d) honesty and transparency; e) other-centredness; f) good intentions with a view to self-correct; g) integrity by delivering as promised; and h) having a long-term view.

**Parkins, J. R., Beckley, T., Comeau, L., Stedman, R. C. Rollins, C. L., & Kessler, A. (2017). Can distrust enhance public engagement? Insights from a national survey on energy issues in Canada.** *Society & Natural Resources, 30* **(8), 934–948.**

This study of 3,000 Canadians explored factors contributing to public engagement on energy issues. The researchers posit that the roles of distrust, scepticism and cynicism, while seemingly negative, are important to public engagement.

**Sherren, K., Beckley, T., Greenland-Smith, S., & Comeau, L. (2017). How provincial and local discourses aligned against the prospect of dam removal in New Brunswick, Canada.** *Water Alternatives, 10* **(3), 697–723.**

Researchers explored the case of public consults surrounding a proposed dam removal in New Brunswick, studying the process of consensus-building between the public and government.

More studies about the process of consensus-building as a function of PR would be valuable, including the unique process with First Nations.

**Tavchar, A. (2017).** *"Are there perks to being a Twitter wallflower? Peripheral participants in a Twitter-enabled learning space in public relations and higher education* **[Dissertation, University of Toronto]. ProQuest Dissertations and Theses Global.**

Surveys, focus groups and interviews were used to investigate low levels of PR student engagement with Twitter at Humber College, with students reporting the feeling that they had 'nothing to say'. Suggestions for encouraging Twitter use by students were proposed.

**Thurlow, A. (2017) Canada – development and expansion of public relations. In T. Watson (Ed.),** *North American perspectives on the development of public relations: Other Voices* **(pp. 37–50). Palgrave Macmillan UK**.

Thurlow formalises the beginnings of discussions about distinctive historical narratives for the development of PR in Canada.

**Thurlow, A., Kushniryk, A., Yue, A. R., Blanchette, K., Murchland, P., & Simon, A. (2017). Evaluating excellence: A model of evaluation for public relations practice in organisational culture and context.** *Public Relations Review*, *43* **(1), 71–79**.

The researchers propose the *Excellence in Organisational Context* model as a new model to measure excellence in practice. The authors tested the model on the Alberta Energy Regulator in a mixed methods approach of interviews and surveys, revealing eight dimensions of excellence.

**Watson, T. (Ed.). (2017).** *North American perspectives on the development of public Relations: Other voices*. **Palgrave Macmillan**.

Watson discusses the history of PR in the United States and Canada. Thurlow describes the development and acceleration of Canadian PR as distinctly separate from the U.S. narrative, particularly around identity, ethics and professionalisation. Wright and Flynn highlight the growing professional standards and university programs in the United States and Canada. Lee, Likely and Valin outline the expansion of government PR in Canada and the United States, which emerged together but under differing political, economic, cultural and legal contexts. Canadian development of PR is categorised into four sections: the interwar period, WWII, the expansive years of the 1950s–1960s and current practice. Discussions in these sections include the growth towards greater scientific approaches, professionalisation and the institutionalisation of the government communications branch in the 2000s. Tilson describes entertainment publicity and its development in the US and Canada; its evolution is argued to be accelerated by secularisation and the rise of celebrity worship within both the movies and sports industries. Gower concludes the volume with her chapter on the historiography of North American PR, identifying gaps and encouraging further historical research into women in PR, particularly as to the impacts and contributions of unhailed women in PR and not just ones deemed to be 'exceptional'.

**Wegner, N. (2017). Discursive battlefields: Support(ing) the troops in Canada.** *International Journal: Canada's Journal of Global Policy Analysis*, *72* **(4), 444–462**.

Wegner argues that discursive emphasis by the Government of Canada on the key message 'support the troops' was used to engender public support for

Canadian military involvement in Afghanistan, 2001–2011. But how much success is too much? Wegner argues that the campaign was so successful that it silenced fulsome anti-war debate.

**2017 Annual Report of the Canadian Veterinary Medical Association. (2018).** *Canadian Veterinary Journal, 59* (7), 724–726.

The association notes the many tactics it uses to communicate with its publics including website, emails, fax, publications, social media (Facebook, Twitter), media pitching, webinar, bilingual videos and monthly electronic newsletters. Rise in social media followers is noted. Various public information campaigns are referenced.

   Public relations around veterinary care has not been researched. Canada is a nation of pet owners with almost as many pets as people. How does public relations work in this profession express itself, considering the mediating factor of personal pets?

**Farmer, Y., Bissière, M., & Benkirane, A. (2018). Impacts of authority and unanimity on social conformity in online chats about climate change.** *Canadian Journal of Communication, 43* (2), 265–279.

Researchers at the Université du Québec à Montréal use a combination of quantitative and qualitative research methods to measure the effects of *unanimity* and *authority* (two variables of persuasive communication) on *social conformity* when strangers communicated in an online forum discussion. The study showed that people are likely to conform to groups when communicating via social media, succumbing to peer pressure. The researchers remind readers that influence, persuasion and conformity are at the heart of persuasion and, therefore, require the application of careful ethical considerations.

**Gauthier, B. (2018).** *Strategic communication in Canada: Planning effective PR campaigns.* **Canadian Scholars**.

Gauthier offers PR students a textbook on campaign strategy, which includes some theoretical underpinnings from critical cultural studies, mass media theory and advertising. Gauthier moves students through thorough situation analysis to execution. Some Canadian distinctives are addressed such as media consumption habits, government communication, Canadian statistics and Canadian examples.

**Gunster, S., & Neubauer, R. (2018). From public relations to mob rule: Media framing of social licence in Canada.** *Canadian Journal of Communication, 43* (1), 11–32.

Researchers tracked the concept of *social licence* in Canadian media by tracing evolutionary use of the term. The term first appeared in 1998 and was dominated by a corporatist perspective until 2012 when the term began to be used in other contexts, such as in the political context, specifically in opposition to pipelines. The authors suggest a typology of usage for the concept: corporate, regulatory, oppositional and conservative attack.

**Heritz, J. (2018). Municipal-Indigenous relations in Saskatchewan: Getting started in Regina, Saskatoon and Prince Albert.** *Canadian Public Administration, 61* **(4), 616–640.**

Heritz examines the political representation of Indigenous Peoples in municipal governance through the concepts of *citizen participation* and *governance interface*. The study was conducted through a qualitative case study of three key municipalities. Results showed that Indigenous representation was based on informal networks. All three municipalities fell below recommended levels of engagement, and they all lacked in Indigenous advisory committees or Indigenous relations offices.

**Kenny, T. (2018).** *IndigiComms: Using decolonization, power studies and Indigenous methods to inform post-modern communications practice and scholarship* **[Unpublished paper, Mount Royal University].**

In this autoethnographic study, Kenny explores Indigenous ways of knowing, attempting to bridge the gap between Indigenous culture and modern PR practice. Kenny includes a discussion of Indigenous images in Canadian history, critical theory, and media framing, ending with a call for more "Warrior Scholars" to champion inclusivity in PR scholarship and practice (p. 23). Kenny poses a *Two-Eyed Seeing Model* that illustrates a view of *IndigiComms* as the intersection of Indigenous studies and public relations/communication studies. Kenny recommends that *IndigiComms* contains the concepts of autoethnography, intersectionality, reflexivity, be grounded in the work of Canada's *Truth and Reconciliation Commission* and involve Indigenous research methods (p. 30). This represents a key, foundational work to the Indigenisation efforts of public relations scholarship and practice.

**McIvor, P. (2018) Creating and implementing a new visual identity: The Halton Healthcare experience.** *Journal of Professional Communication,* **5(2), 99–106.**

This case study explores a Toronto hospital's process in adopting a new visual brand identity across three facilities in several communities utilising an iterative approach involving multiple stakeholders. The uniqueness of such a study is the Canadian context of a government-funded healthcare system. A communication audit and attitude analysis was employed to produce an award-winning visual identity.

Szustaczek, C., Kikkert, P., Knudsen, C., & Dreighton, J. (2018). Sheridan@50: A creative history for a creative campus. *Journal of Professional Communication*, 6 (1), 165–174.

This is a case study of a 50th anniversary celebration and its communication strategies. The strategy included a documentary, travelling display, social media campaign, web page, events, print and digital publications. This is a practical paper that could serve as a point of examination in a classroom. The campaign helped to document the college's history and build awareness.

Thurlow, A., Sevigny, A., & Dottori, M. (2018, February). Global capabilities in public relations. *Public Relations Journal*, 11 (3), 1–27.

Researchers provide some insights into the first phase of the *Global Capability Project*, a study of PR capabilities across nine countries. A Delphi panel of 14 Canadian academics, practitioners and executives were asked to identify key capabilities of successful PR practice, with 10 common core capabilities being identified, among other findings. Phase Two will attempt to validate these findings through a cross-Canada survey of practitioners. This is an extensive study that digs deep into aspects of Canadian practice.

Thurlow, A., Kushniryk, A., Blotnicky, K., & Yue, A. R. (2018). Roles, decision-making, and access to the dominant coalition: The practice of public relations in Canada. *Journal of Professional Communication*, 5 (2), 41–58.

This is the first Canadian edition of the *GAP Study* developed by the University of Southern California, and is based on 197 surveys. The findings show that Canadian practitioners report higher rates of access to the dominant coalition. They also express higher rates of optimism in terms of their efficacy and impact on their organisations, suggesting greater control, particularly in the area of social media. Women in Canadian PR are very well qualified and often work in nonprofit or government agencies; yet, they are paid less than their male counterparts. The researchers suggest that the glass ceiling in the Canadian context requires further research, particularly since women in Canada report greater access to the dominant coalition but are not compensated accordingly. An area identified for improvement in the field is program measurement and evaluation.

Tisch, D. (2018). Thirty percent off Ontario tuition: A student engagement problem. *Journal of Professional Communication*, 5 (2), 107–116.

Tisch, of Argyle Public Relations, worked with a government ministry to promote a tuition rebate program for post-secondary students. After research, Tisch employed a strategy of peer-to-peer communication, having ministry representatives on campuses to pre-qualify students, and integration with social media. The program reached 29,000 students across 47 campuses within 21 days and realised a 27.5% increase in registrations for the program. Tisch noted that a key learning from the campaign was that students, while a single target public, are not homogenous (e.g., Indigenous, married, mature) and have a range of needs and questions. Having a government official on hand to deal with unique needs was noted as a key success factor.

**Wood, T. (2018). Energy's citizens: The making of a Canadian petro-public.** *Canadian Journal of Communication, 43* (1).

Wood attempts to discover the methods and motives of this petroleum group and its supporters, calling their efforts a form of *astroturfing*. He traces the association's history, the political environment, the communications efforts and recruitment strategies to increase membership of the group. Wood concluded the primary motive for the effort was to provide tools for its strongest supporters to amplify its message.

**Achor, P. N., & Nnabuko, J. O. (2019). Quasi-gatekeeping and quasi-gatewatching: The dual role of public relations practitioners in the social media domain.** *Canadian Journal of Communication, 44* (1), 5–24.

The researchers introduce the terms *quasi-gatekeeping* and *quasi-gatewatching* as part of the information management function by PR workers as they utilise social media. Researchers highlight the loss of control social media managers can sometimes experience and identify *blocking messaging* or *deleting parties* as regulation methods. Also, PR practitioners can still exert control by managing their own content choices and postings on their own channels.

## References

Emms, M. J. (1995). *The origins of public relations as an occupation in Canada* [Masters Dissertation, Concordia University, Montreal].

Kugler, M. (2004). *Des campagnes de communication réussies. 43 études de cas primés*. Presses de l'Université du Québec.

# 6 2020s

- Interest in government communications remains a recurring theme, along with ongoing interest in crisis communications (largely in a government context), which had emerged in the prior decade.
- PR scholarship in the Canadian context begins to appear more consistently in Canadian-based communications research outlets.

**Bannerman, S. (2020).** *Canadian communication policy and law.* **Canadian Scholars**.

This textbook integrates theory and practice by examining Canadian communication law. It provides a companion piece to Lemon and Sing (2015) who discuss freedom of expression, honesty in advertising, intellectual property, copyright, trademarks, privacy and freedom of information. Bannerman covers similar material but integrates aspects of critical theory and power dynamics behind legal and policy decisions.

**Banyongen, S. (2020). Assessing crisis communication teamwork performance during a terrorist attack: A pragma-dialectic analysis.** *Canadian Journal of Communication, 45* **(3), 437–462**.

Banyongen examines government crisis communication around the shooting incident at the Canadian National War Memorial in 2014 against best practices in strategic crisis leadership. The researcher focuses on the media relations aspect, specifically a key press conference.

Banyongen poses an interesting research approach, suggesting the press conference as a unit of study.

**Braun, S. L. (2020).** *Public relations as public diplomacy: The Royal Bank of Canada's monthly letter, 1943–2003.* **Routledge**.

This monograph is a case study of the Royal Bank of Canada's *Monthly Letter*, which was initially created in 1920 as a traditional economic newsletter written by an economist but became a global public relations tool beginning

DOI: 10.4324/9781003507475-9

in 1943 when it came under the influence of publicist John Heron. This is an in-depth theoretical examination of the concepts of *public relations* as *public diplomacy* in which the author likens the two concepts as 'two sides of the same coin'.

Chen, R. (2020). The stakeholder-communication continuum: An alternate approach to internal and external communications. *Journal of Professional Communication, 6* (1), 7–33.

The researcher proposes a theoretical framework of a stakeholder-communication continuum as a way to accurately capture the university-alumni relationship, with internal communication on one end and external communication on the other, positing that university alumni are both internal and external stakeholders simultaneously.

Dobosz, S. (2020). Crisis, communication, and Canadian hospitals: An analysis and evaluation of risk preparedness and crisis communication efforts of Ontario hospitals. *Canadian Journal of Communication, 45* (3), 365–385.

Fourteen communications practitioners from Ontario hospitals were interviewed about the state of risk preparedness and crisis communications in their respective hospital systems. The author points out that there have been few studies of crisis communications in hospitals and none in Canada. The study reveals the high levels of trust by Canadians in their national systems, specifically the healthcare system. Studies about public relations in the Canadian medical environment would contribute to the field of health communications.

Gateman, M. (2020). *'Success' stories, government public relations, and the resettlement of South East Asian Refugees in Canada 1979–1980* [Masters thesis, Dalhousie University].

Gateman argues that although the Canadian Employment and Emigration department produced a newsletter, *The Indochinese Refugees' Newsletter*, to disseminate positive information about refugee resettlement in Canada among this group of refugees during the period, public opinion was not as favourable as the government depicted. Gateman examined the 21 issues of the newsletter, exploring the narratives and themes of the newsletter.

Kelleher, T., & Males, A. M. (2020). *Public relations* (Canadian ed.). Oxford University Press.

This textbook is a primer for students of public relations and includes fulsome treatment of digital media and new technologies. Canadian distinctives include a discussion of Canadian law, the *Canadian Charter of Rights and*

*Freedom*s, the CRTC and the *Canadian Human Rights Act*, as well as public relations ethics as outlined by CPRS. The book is now in its second edition. (See Kelleher, 2021.)

**Koerber, D. (2020). Connecting crisis communication theory and Canadian communication research.** *Canadian Journal of Communication, 45* (3), 359–363.

This issue of the journal is dedicated to crisis communications cases in Canada. Koerber, serving as editor, notes the purpose of the issue was to develop Canadian-based content. The contexts of these case studies are hospitals/healthcare, social media for disaster-preparedness and political communication. Koerber notes the need to look at crisis through "a Canadian lens" (p. 363).

Koerber hints that some socio-cultural aspects of Canadian practise likely exist and require study.

**Leadbetter, K. (2020). Reputation and social capital: A hammer for the glass ceiling.** *Journal of Professional Communication, 6* (1), 35–70.

This is a case study of a women's professional network, examining the efficacy of networking to advancement. Results reveal that networks can contribute to leadership in the form of social capital and reputation enhancement. However, the network needs to have relationship-building components such as mentorship programs.

Studies that examine networking more closely could help to advance gender equality at the highest levels of public relations leadership.

**Mosher, A. (2020). Healthy discourse: How Canadian physicians use Twitter to communicate in healthcare.** *Journal of Professional Communication, 6* (1), 71–91.

This study provides a benchmark of how and why Canadian physicians use social media. Results revealed that Canadian physicians use Twitter for a) professional development; b) to influence health policy; and c) to raise health awareness and health literacy. They were not focused on social media for the economics of practice. Interesting research questions arise: In a medical system that is government-funded, how do medical professionals in Canada view or practise public relations? What is the role of public relations in the Canadian doctor-patient relationship, and how is it expressed?

**Oldring, A., Milekhina, A., & Brand, A. (2020). Tweeting tsunami: Influence and early warning in British Columbia.** *Canadian Journal of Communication, 45* (3), 387–409.

The researchers examine the use of social media as an early warning system, applying it to a Canadian context through the use of Twitter. Using social network analysis, content analysis and surveys, researchers concluded that Twitter was a viable way to locate early warning stakeholders in at-risk areas.

The exploration of social media for large-scale crisis communication is an ongoing topic of interest in the Canadian context considering the vastness of the geography, the diversity of social media platforms, the diversity of users and the many remote areas in the nation.

**Sévigny,, A., & Lamonica, T. (2020). 10 Tips for strategic public relations during the COVID-19 pandemic. *Journal of Professional Communication, 6* (1), 179–184.**

This paper offers 10 tips for strategic communication during the ongoing pandemic, based on a study conducted by Léger and McMaster Master of Communication Management Research Lab.

**Siddiqi, S., & Koerber, D. (2020). The anatomy of a national crisis: The Canadian federal government's response to the 2015 Kurdi refugee case. *Canadian Journal of Communication, 45* (3), 411–435.**

Researchers examine the Government of Canada's response to news coverage of a Syrian boy who lost his life on a beach in Turkey while fleeing war, revealing government responses adhered to best practices.

**Versailles, G. (2020). Journalism and public relations. *Journal of Professional Communication, 6* (1), 93–163.**

Versailles argues that journalistic training enhances public relations work, based on his personal experiences in both fields. He makes the observation that francophone media are more strident and militant in their journalistic approaches than anglophone media.

Some cross-pollination of PR research, observations, comparison and contrast between French and English resources are needed to bridge those gaps and produce a holistic view of PR research, practice and scholarship in the Canadian context.

**Hier, S. P. (2021). A moral panic in reverse? Implicatory denial and COVID-19 pre-crisis risk communication in Canada. *Canadian Journal of Communication, 46* (3), 505–521.**

Presenting an overview of the crisis response by the health policymakers in Canada in the early period of COVID-19, the researcher argues that the Canadian government largely under-reacted to the crisis in the forms of poor communication, mixed messaging and contradictions.

Critical examination of government responses to COVID-19 remains largely under-explored from a public relations perspective.

**Homburg, V., & Moody, R. (2021). "@Government There's a pothole in my street!": Canadian citizens' adoption choices of social media use in citizen-government relations.** *Canadian Public Administration, 64* **(4), 631–656.**

Researchers conducted an online survey to determine motivations and attitudes of Canadians when engaging in digital conversation with government agencies. Quantitative analysis of 309 responses revealed that a) citizens were more likely to respond to government communications if they trusted the social media platform being used; and b) citizens who felt their digital responses would have some effect indicated were more likely to use social media to communicate with government.

With Canada having a propensity toward government systems, research into government communications contributes to the national distinctiveness.

**Jekanowski, R. W. (2021). From Labrador to Leipzig: Film and infra-structures along the Fur Trail.** *Canadian Journal of Communication, 46* **(2), 291–314.**

Since 1919, the Hudson's Bay Company has used the medium of film to capture its history. The researcher examines some 140 films at the company's archives for the narratives of colonialism and Settler expansionism.

The role of film, particularly historically, has not been broadly examined through the lens of public relations, other than some isolated works around war propaganda.

**Ju, R., Dong, C., & Zhang, Y. (2021). How controversial businesses communicate CSR on Facebook: Insights from the Canadian cannabis industry.** *Public Relations Review, 47* **(4).**

Through the use of content analysis, researchers explore CSR and the use of social media for product promotion by the cannabis industry. Findings suggested that the CSR communication was promotional (focused on economic motives) and lacked transparency, which the researchers note as posing an ethical dilemma for marketers.

**CPRS. (2021, March).** *PR profession: Diversity, equity and inclusion study.* **Léger Company. Report No: 82654–048. www.cprs.ca/About/News/2021-(1)/Canada%E2%80%99s-PR-industry-releases-first-comprehensive**

This is the first study of its kind, conducted by Léger for the Canadian Council of Public Relations firms, CPRS and IABC. Data from a sample of 1,231

Canadian communications professionals benchmark key findings around DEI in Canadian practice. Key findings include the following: a) While diversity is present, ethnic and gender diversity diminishes at top levels; b) current employers are reported to have largely inclusive environments; c) many racialized professionals and women report incidents of discrimination; and d) there is a gender gap with regard to health issues, among other findings. This is a key industry report on the status of the field.

**Lindell, D. J. (2021). Brands vs babies: Paid content and authenticity in Canadian mommy blogs.** *Journal of Professional Communication, 6* (2), 63–85.

A quantitative content analysis of 290 Canadian blog posts suggests that the use of paid content threatens authenticity, transparency and disclosure by bloggers. The researcher encourages greater transparency in the form of disclosure as a means to retain integrity and credibility.

**Neubauer, R., & Graham, N. (2021). Fuelling the subsidized public: Mapping the flow of extractivist content on Facebook.** *Canadian Journal of Communication, 46* (4), 905–938.

The authors conducted a network analysis of six pro-oil advocacy groups active on Facebook to discover information flows and the sharing of social media content to amplify common narratives and messaging.

**Bryukhanova, H. (2022). Analysis of basic education concepts in Ukraine and Canada (in the field "advertising and public relations").** *Educational Challenges, 27* (1), 47–54.

The researcher compares public relations terminology and research concepts around professional training and education in the domains of advertising and public relations across the Ukrainian and Canadian contexts, revealing distinct approaches. The researcher felt such knowledge could be used in the systematisation of the accumulated scientific knowledge in the field.

There has been a movement for global approaches and systematisation of public relations practice and education. This study supports findings that it is possible to globalise certain elements of public relations education and professionalisation; however, cultural aspects appear to mitigate.

**Devries, M. (2022). Archetypes and homophilic avatars: New approaches to studying Far-Right Facebook practice.** *Canadian Journal of Communication, 47* (1), 151–171.

Devries finds that individuals are more likely to engage in 'far-right' politics on Facebook based on the social groups to which they belong, rather than on individual psychology.

**LaVigne, M. H., Babiuk, C., & Jarjoura, B. (Eds.). (2022). *Internal communications in Canada*. Rocks Mills Press.**

This edited book is well-grounded in both organisational theory and also public relations principles to support the sub-field of internal communications. It includes research, case studies and issues in DEI. This is a unique and specialised textbook suitable for use within a public relations program of study.

**MacKenzie, L. (2022). Public relations responsiveness during crime spikes: How and to what extent do social media and news-reporting exacerbate liquor-store thefts in Winnipeg? *The McMaster Journal of Communication*, *13* (1), 41–87.**

This case study explored if and how social media posts and media reports contributed to a spree of liquor thefts in Winnipeg. The relationship between news media, police and citizens were explored, primarily through *Balance Zone Theory*.

**Sharp, C. M. (2022). Shell is proud to present . . . the spirit sings': Museum sponsorship and public relations in oil country. *Museum & Society*, *20* (2), 172–189.**

Sharp takes a critical look at sponsorships and museum exhibits by examining a controversial exhibit that attracted 150 protestors to Calgary's Glenbow Museum during the 1988 Olympics. Protestors mainly objected to exhibit sponsorship by Shell Canada. Sharp examines this protest as a case study using the theoretical lens of corporate legitimation. Discussions around political, economic and historical considerations reveal the complexity of museum exhibitions in energy-based cities.

**Joseph, K., & McNally, M. B. (2023). Framing issues: Public participation in Canadian Wireless Spectrum Consultations. *Canadian Journal of Communication*, *48* (2), p. 307–342.**

Researchers explore the public consultation process of telecommunication industry regulators to reveal low levels of public participation in favour of high levels of industry participation. Researchers argue that the low public participation delegitimizes the regulators and calls for reform.

**Petry, R. A. (2023). Altering regional development for sustainability: Lessons learned from strategic communications of RCE Saskatchewan (Canada) with government. *Frontiers in Sustainability (Lausanne)*, *3*.**

This paper explores the role of strategic letter writing by a nonprofit group to influence governmental decisions toward specific actions around mining, agriculture and forestry, among others. Utilising nine successful educational letters addressed to various levels of Saskatchewan government by the non-profit, the researcher identifies key success factors of the letters.

## References

Kelleher, T. (2021). *Public relations* (Canadian Edition, 2nd ed.). Oxford University Press.

Lemon, D., & Sing, C. (2015). Communications and marketing law in Canada. In W. W. Carney & L. A. Lymer (Eds.), *Fundamentals of public relations and marketing communications in Canada* (pp. 39–57). Pica Press.

# Part Three

# Conclusion

# 7 Conclusions and Future Implications

## Observations

Specific observations have been noted at the beginning of each chapter and within annotations. Therefore, this will be a general summation of important highlights.

Development of PR research in Canada is only in its beginnings. Earliest works appeared haphazardly in non-communications-oriented journals. The first article in a PR journal was Wright's (1976) *Public Relations Quarterly*, which was a discussion of U.S.-Canadian differentiation. The first modern, empirical study published in a communications journal appeared in *Public Relations Review* and was a survey of Canadian female practitioners (Scrimger, 1985). Relevant articles were scattered, thereafter, across both non-communications journals and communications journals.

Scholarship became more consistent with the advent of the *McMaster Journal of Communication* in 2009 and a sister publication, the *Journal of Professional Communication* in 2011. Canada's premier scholarly communications journal, the *Canadian Journal of Communication*, began to publish more articles, commensurately, leading with a key article about the Maple Foods listeriosis crisis in 2009, but it has not served as a primary outlet for PR scholarship in the Canadian context, by comparison.

One Canadian distinctive that has emerged as a result of this research is that student-scholars have played a particularly important role in the development of scholarship, along with industry-scholars. (The *Journal of Professional Communication* invites articles from industry representatives.) This reliance on student-scholars and industry-scholars, rather than traditional academics, is a rather unique feature in Canada's PR scholarship story.

While all of these developments represent progress in research, the nature of that research is dominated by small-scale studies, case studies and qualitative methodologies, which are limited for their generalisability. More empirical studies are needed to elevate the field.

DOI: 10.4324/9781003507475-11

## Emerging Themes From Existing Research

Government communication – As noted in some of the chapter summaries, Canada is noted by its interest in government processes and communications. All levels of government have been studied – federal, provincial and municipal – with the earliest published work written by a government official on the topic of forestry conservation (Dickson, 1933). Related contexts such as government-industry partnerships, NGOs and international branding have also been explored. This interest has remained constant over the decades and contributes a distinctiveness to the Canadian PR research narrative. This trend may be a reflection of a Canadian view of PR more as public communication in the public sphere or for public interest, more in keeping with the European view of PR; this is worthy of some exploration (Bentele & Nothhaft, 2010).

Crisis communications studies and discussion are popular – Next to government communication, studies of crisis communication were consistently popular. The *Journal of Professional Communication*, for example, dedicated an entire issue to the topic in 2012, with three out of six articles set in Canadian contexts. This is likely to remain of high interest. To advance scholarship in this area, more examination of Flynn's (2006) *Balance Zone Theory*, or other approaches, can be utilised.

History – More biographies of those well known and not so well known, across all PR sectors, would add to the Canadian story. Additionally, more work needs to be done to document the trajectory of PR historical development, building on the foundation of Emms (1995).

Issues of national identity and character – Canada has been historically plagued by the question, "What is Canadian?" This theme has also emerged in PR scholarship. Issues of cultural identity and culture in practice can be explored. Some hints have emerged; perhaps there, indeed, exists a strong vein of dialogue, two-way symmetry and collaboration as some researchers have suggested. And new approaches need to be developed in light of generous immigration policies and the rising immigrant population. Examination into ethnic PR agencies would be timely and revealing about the changing face of Canada and the world in which communicators operate.

Decolonisation – A recent theme, and a distinctive one, revolves around decolonisation. Most pointedly in this case, reference must be made to the challenge put forward by Canada's Truth and Reconciliation Commission (2015) to societal institutions, including post-secondary institutions. With respect to the issue of Indigenous issues, a body of research is developing to support the decolonisation of scholarship. (See McGregor et al., 2018; Huaman & Martin, 2023; Datta, 2023.). While there has not been extensive work with respect to decolonisation within PR scholarship in Canada, it is emerging (Kenny, 2018).

The emerging Canadian contexts – PR within the Canadian context is beginning to be studied and acknowledged more, as evidenced by the accelerating number of relevant textbooks containing Canadian examples. Additionally, many studies have been emerging in the formal research literature, particularly since 2009.

## Other Future Research Considerations

In addition to the themes and questions posed earlier, the following also emerge as possible future research considerations:

- The intersection of PR and religion has not been explored to the same depth or degree as in the U.S. context. (See, for example, Lamme, 2014.)
- PR and the arts have not been widely studied.
- PR and contested geopolitical spaces can propel us toward distinct narratives. For example, Canada is a nation of two official languages – English and French. The development of PR within the francophone context is acknowledged in this monograph by the inclusion of available French texts; however, PR processes at work across the French-English dynamic have yet to be explored, as well as cross-translation of texts and materials.
- Research into the role of PR in other contested spaces such as East-West relations or Settler-Indigenous issues can also be studied through the lens of PR and contribute to a distinct narrative. Other narratives could likely include themes around a) political issues (e.g., Riel Rebellion, separatist movements, regional independence issues); c) impacts of immigration and intercultural communication with Canada's generous immigration policies; d) ever-shifting politics; e) the impact of geography on practice; f) U.S. and Canadian relations and the Americanisation of PR; g) Canada as a mosaic rather than a melting pot – myth or fact? Contextualizing PR around some of these unique forces and incidents can bring forward new and distinct narratives that illuminate the country and its people.
- The development of PR education in Canada has not been well studied, including comparative and critical approaches.

## Challenges

Clearly, the study of PR practice and history in Canada is underdeveloped, mainly due to a lack of numbers of graduate programs, few scholars dedicated to this work and limited funding. Industry-scholars have been one source of development, as has been mentioned, and this could be nurtured. However, the future of scholarly development, for Canada, lies primarily with student-scholars. Graduate students from the few programs that exist, or senior undergraduate students from baccalaureate programs, are needed to provide the labour necessary for research development. Student-scholars have been extremely important to the progression of research thus far. They will be needed en masse to provide the seeds and root systems by which future research seeds can germinate, grow and ultimately flourish.

## References

Bentele, G., & Nothhaft, H. (2010). Strategic communication and the public sphere from a European perspective. *International Journal of Strategic Communication, 4*(2), 93–116.

Datta, R. (Ed.). (2023). *Decolonization in practice: Reflective learning from cross-cultural perspectives*. Canadian Scholars.

Dickson, J. R. (1933). The development of public opinion in relation to forest reservation in Canada. *Empire Forestry Journal, 12*(2), 215–228.

Emms, M. J. (1995). *The origins of public relations as an occupation in Canada* [Master's Thesis, Concordia University, Montreal].

Flynn, T. (2006). A delicate equilibrium: Balancing theory, practice and outcomes. *Journal of Public Relations Research, 18*(2), 191–201.

Huaman, E. S., & Martin, N. D. (Eds.). (2023). *Indigenous research design: Transnational perspectives in practice*. Canadian Scholars.

Kenny, T. (2018). *IndigiComms: Using decolonization, power studies and Indigenous methods to inform post-modern communications practice and scholarship* [Unpublished paper, Mount Royal University, Calgary, Canada].

Lamme, M. (2014). *Public relations and religion in American history: Evangelism, temperance and business*. Routledge

McGregor, D., Restoule, J. P., & Johnston, R. (Eds.). (2018). *Indigenous research: Theories, practice and relationships*. Canadian Scholars.

Scrimger, J. (1985). Profile: Women in Canadian PR. *Public Relations Review, 11*(3), 40–46.

Truth and Reconciliation Commission of Canada. (2015). *Calls to action*. https://publications.gc.ca/site/eng/9.801236/publication.html

Wright, N. K. (1976). The challenge of public relations in Canada. *Public Relations Quarterly, 21*(3), 23–25.

# Appendix

## Canadian Textbooks and Pedagogical Resources

Bannerman, S. (2020). *Canadian communication policy and law*. Canadian Scholars.

Cardin, M., & McMullan, K. (2015). *Canadian PR for the real world*. Pearson.

Carney, W. W., Babiuk, C., & LaVigne, M. H. (2019). *In the news: The practice of media relations in Canada* (3rd ed.). University of Alberta Press.

Carney, W. W., & Lymer, L. A. (Eds.). (2015). *Fundamentals of public relations and marketing communications in Canada*. Pica Press.

Cooper, J. (2015). *Crisis communications in Canada: A practical approach* (2nd ed.). Centennial College Press.

Dumas, M. (2010). *Les relations publiques, une profession en devenir*. Presses de l'Université du Québec.

Fleras, A. (2003). *Mass media communication in Canada*. Top Hat.

Gasher, M., Skinner, D., & Coulter, N. (2020). *Media and communication in Canada: Networks, culture, technology, audiences* (9th ed.). Oxford University Press.

Gauthier, B. (2018). *Strategic communication in Canada: Planning effective PR campaigns*. Canadian Scholars.

Hacker, D., & Sommers, N. (2021). *A Canadian writer's reference* (7th ed.). Bedford/St. Martin's.

Kelleher, T. (2021). *Public relations* (Canadian Edition, 2nd ed.). Oxford University Press.

Koerber, D. (2017). *Crisis communication in Canada*. University of Toronto Press.

Kugler, M. (2004). *Des campagnes de communication réussies. 43 études de cas primés*. Presses de l'Université du Québec.

Kugler, M. (2010). *Des campagnes de communication réussies, Tome 2: 42 études de cas primés*. Presses de l'Université du Québec.

LaVigne, M. H. (2020). *Proactive media relations: A Canadian perspective*. Centennial College Press.

LaVigne, M. H., Babiuk, C., & Jarjoura, B. (Eds.). (2022). *Internal communications in Canada*. Rocks Mills Press.

Lorimer, R., Gasher, M., & Skinner, D. (2017). *Mass communication in Canada* (8th ed.). Langara College.

Maisonneuve, D. (2010). *Les relations publiques dans une société en mouvance* (4e éd.). PUQ.

Marland, A., Giasson, T., & Small, T. (Eds.). (2015). *Political communication in Canada: Meet the press and Tweet the rest*. UBC Press.

McCarten, J. (Ed.). (2021). *The Canadian Press stylebook* (19th ed.). Canadian Press.

McCarten, J. (Ed.). (2022). *The Canadian Press caps and spelling* (23rd ed.). Canadian Press.

McKie, C., & Singer, B. D. (2001). *Communications in Canadian society* (5th ed.). Thompson Educational.

Parsons, P. (2016). *Ethics in public relations: A guide to best practice* (3rd ed.). Kogan Press.

Shade, L. R. (2014). *Mediascapes: New patterns in Canadian communication* (4th ed.). Nelson.

Shiller, Ed. (1994). *The Canadian guide to managing the media* (Revised ed.). Prentice Hall.

Sommers, S. (2009). *Building media relationships: How to establish, maintain and develop long-term relationships with the media* (2nd ed.). Oxford University Press.

Stokes, J. (2016). *The complete all-Canadian content writing handbook*. United States Blurb Incorporated.

Vipond, M. (2011). *Mass media in Canada* (4th ed.). James Lorimer & Company, Ltd.

For Product Safety Concerns and Information please contact our EU
representative  GPSR@taylorandfrancis.com
Taylor & Francis Verlag GmbH, Kaufingerstraße 24, 80331 München, Germany

www.ingramcontent.com/pod-product-compliance
Ingram Content Group UK Ltd.
Pitfield, Milton Keynes, MK11 3LW, UK
UKHW021822240425
457818UK00006B/38